D0930242

SOUP NIGHTS

For Emily Bell,

with gratitude for your friendship
and admiration for
your extraordinary creativity.

SOUP NIGHTS

SATISFYING SOUPS

AND SIDES

FOR DELICIOUS MEALS

ALL YEAR

BY BETTY ROSBOTTOM

PHOTOGRAPHS BY HARRY ZERNIKE

RIZZOLI
NEW YORK

New York · Paris · London · Milan

CONTENTS

SOUP AGAIN
WITH NO APOLOGY

BEFORE WRITING THE PROPOSAL for this book, I asked myself, "Why another soup book?" Indeed, there are countless volumes on the subject, including one I authored several years ago. Nevertheless, my mind was racing with ideas for all the new soups I might create, and all the familiar ones that I could reinvent. The truth is that I've been addicted to soup since I took my first sip as a youngster. And, from teaching countless cooking classes over the years, I have learned from students that soup never goes out of fashion and happily adapts to even the most demanding lifestyles. So without another hesitation, I set out on another soup journey.

Why are soups so adored? There are so many reasons: They are generally easy to prepare yet satisfying. They are forgiving if we make an error or two. They don't break the bank. They are comforting and homey, and endlessly versatile. Add to this their make-ahead advantages, and it's easy to see why soup has never gone out of style in the home kitchen.

As I worked on this book, the constant refrain from my friends, students, and neighbors was "I lo-o-o-o-ve soup!" In today's hyper-competitive world, where logic and data are supposed to supersede passion and emotion, confessing that I chose to feature soups once again because of their sentimental, consoling, and heartening appeal might not sound convincing. But these were the very reasons I relished every minute, hour, day, and month creating these recipes. Soups reward us with a certain joie de vivre too often absent in our frenetic daily lives.

Writing another soup book was like reinventing the little black dress—take something familiar and beloved, then add creative touches to freshen and give it new life. And that is exactly what I have tried to do in this collection: I've added twists to classics and invented new preparations.

As a cooking teacher and longtime cookbook author, I know how important it is to make a book user-friendly. I've divided soups by type— vegetable-driven, fish soups, soups with beans and grains, hearty soups for countering cold weather, and chilled and lighter ones for warmer days. Salads and sandwiches, soup's natural partners, have their own chapters, both brimming with seasonally focused creations. And since I admit to having a sweet tooth, I've made certain that you'll find plenty of choices when it comes to dessert. Think of these sides as carefully selected accessories to that little black dress. In the back of the book, there is a chapter on kitchen basics, including recipes for both homemade stocks and enriched purchased stocks, as well as cooking tips and ingredient notes to guide you when preparing them.

At the end of each soup recipe I've included a menu suggesting a salad or sandwich (sometimes both) and a dessert or two to serve as part of a soup night supper. But I hope readers will delve in and create their own menus as well. Since the side dishes in this collection were all carefully crafted to complement the soups, everything can be easily mixed and matched according to individual taste.

I have spent almost all of my adult life in the food world—as a cooking teacher, a syndicated columnist, a food writer, an author, a local television host, a blogger, and a guide for culinary tours, especially in Europe. These enriching experiences have influenced my cooking, and most certainly the recipes in this book. You'll see many references to Paris and France, where I spend part of every year with my husband, a professor whose research is fortuitously concentrated in those gastronomic epicenters. I grew up in the South and attended college in New Orleans—and these rich culinary heritages of my youth are also reflected in several dishes. For the past two decades my home has been in New England, where an abundance of fresh seafood as well as artisanal cheeses, fresh meats, and heirloom vegetables from local farms are daily temptations. These regional ingredients have often been the inspiration for the soups, sides, or desserts in this book.

Zuppas, brodos, potages, gumbos, chilies, bisques, chowders—the world over, soups are part of every home cook's repertoire and often bring back warm memories of family and place. I vividly recall the tomato gazpacho I served several young American friends in Paris on a sweltering July night when the temperature reached 103 degrees—the icy soup cooled our group down and inspired spirited conversation until midnight. A bouillabaisse that I recreated in my New England home brings back joyful images of Provence, where my husband I have spent many summer vacations. A hearty bean and greens soup with mounds of brown rice created and shared by my longtime colleague, Emily Bell, was delicious on a frosty fall night at her house several years ago. Now when I prepare this soup, it reminds me of our friendship.

My hope is that these and the many other recipes in this collection will encourage you to turn to soup as an incomparable centerpiece for simpler but memorable meals.

—BETTY ROSBOTTOM *Paris, January 2016*

ROASTED BUTTERNUT
SQUASH SOUP *with sage cream*

"SMOOTH AS SILK" PARSNIP
BISQUE

CAULIFLOWER SOUP *with*
toasted hazelnuts and Gruyère

ROASTED CARROT, PARSNIP,
AND GARLIC SOUP

BROCCOLI SOUP
with curried crème fraîche

CREAM OF CELERY ROOT
SOUP *with celery leaf*
and hazelnut gremolata

CALDO VERDE

CREAMY ARTICHOKE SOUP
with lemon and tarragon

WINTER TOMATO AND
GARLIC SOUP *with creamy*
gorgonzola bruschette

BRODO *with fresh peas, mint,*
and pancetta

BRODO *with asparagus, gnocchi,*
and blue cheese

1

WARMING VEGETABLE SOUPS

ON SATURDAY MORNINGS in our small New England town, you'll find me reaching for my big straw basket, searching for my keys, and then heading out to the farmers market. Open from spring to late fall, this market is a welcome beginning to the weekend. Farmers bring crops picked hours earlier, cheesemakers and yogurt producers set up booths with their artisanal products, as do bakers. Gardeners tempt you with their bounty of herbs and flowers. No matter the season, by the time I leave, my basket is overflowing with fresh produce, such as tender asparagus spears and plump green peas in the spring or deep golden butternut squash and hearty collards in the fall. These market forays have inspired many of the recipes in this vegetable-driven chapter.

Some of these soups are pureed and enriched with touches of cream or crème fraîche, redolent of the silken smooth French veloutés I've sampled during my frequent stays in France. Roasted Butternut Squash Soup with Sage Cream, Creamy Artichoke Soup with Lemon and Tarragon, and Broccoli Soup with Curried Crème Fraiche are all pureed soups that I have tried to lighten without sacrificing the creaminess (that makes these potages so comforting) by using smaller additions of rich dairy products. Other recipes—such as the Roasted Carrot, Parsnip, and Garlic Soup and the Brodo with Asparagus, Gnocchi, and Blue Cheese—are chunky and filled with texture. In these creations, a colorful mélange of vegetables floats in the flavorful broth of each bowl.

Most of the soups in this chapter are made with vegetables alone, though a few—the Brodo with Fresh Peas, Mint, and Pancetta and Caldo Verde, a classic Portuguese soup prepared with collards, potatoes, and sliced chorizo—have accents of smoky meats to complement their flavor.

Today's cooks don't have to look far to find farmers markets and roadside stands selling local produce. And even at supermarkets, vegetable shopping has become much more exciting. I often spend the better part of my visits in the produce aisle. The selection of readily available greens has expanded exponentially, enticing cooks with chard, kale, and collards. Items like knobby celery root, mushrooms of infinite varieties, and many other rediscovered vegetables now share shelf space with workaday carrots, celery, and cauliflower. These additions are more than reason enough to fill your cart and turn your purchases into mouthwatering soups like the ones that follow.

ROASTED BUTTERNUT SQUASH SOUP
WITH SAGE CREAM

PREP TIME	**START-TO-FINISH**	**MAKE AHEAD**
15 minutes	*1 hour, 15 minutes*	*Yes*

IN THE FALL AND WINTER, *I seem to bump into squash soups everywhere. There's no end to their popularity nor their versatility. I am crazy about this version in which golden butternut squash is roasted to intensify its flavor, then simmered in broth and puréed. What really gives this dish a big flavor boost, though, is a final addition of warm crème fraîche that has been infused with sage.*

ARRANGE A RACK AT CENTER POSITION of oven and preheat to 400°F. Line a large, heavy baking sheet with foil and spread the cubed squash on it. Drizzle cubes with oil, and season with 3/4 teaspoon salt and 1/2 teaspoon pepper. Toss cubes to coat with oil and seasonings.

BAKE SQUASH, stirring every 10 minutes to prevent sticking, until tender and lightly browned, 30 to 35 minutes. Watch carefully to make certain it does not burn. Remove from oven.

PLACE CRÈME FRAÎCHE AND DRIED SAGE LEAVES in a medium saucepan over medium heat. Stir to combine and bring to a simmer. Remove from heat and let stand 10 to 15 minutes while the sage infuses the cream.

HEAT BUTTER in a large, heavy pot (with a lid) over medium heat. When hot, add shallots and cook, stirring, until softened and translucent, about 3 minutes. Stir in the squash, add the broth, and bring mixture to a simmer. Cover and simmer until vegetables are very tender, about 10 minutes. Purée soup in batches in a food processor, blender, or food mill, then return to the pot. (Or use an immersion blender to purée the soup in the pot.)

WHISK in 1/2 cup of the crème fraîche. Taste soup and season with additional salt if needed. (Soup can be prepared one day ahead. Cook to this stage, then cool, cover, and refrigerate. Reheat over low heat, stirring. Cover and refrigerate 1/4 cup remaining crème fraîche separately; stir well before using.)

LADLE soup into bowls. Sprinkle each serving with Gruyère and a drizzle of the remaining crème fraîche. If desired, garnish each bowl with a sage sprig.

4 CUPS (about 2 lb) butternut squash, peeled, seeded, and cut into 1-inch dice *(or purchase same quantity of pre-cut squash)*

2 TBSP olive oil

Kosher salt

Freshly ground black pepper

3/4 CUP crème fraîche *see page 201*

1 1/2 TSP dried rubbed sage leaves

2 TBSP unsalted butter

3/4 CUP chopped shallots

4 CUPS chicken broth or stock *(or Homemade Vegetable Stock, page 199)*

1/2 CUP grated Gruyère

4 fresh sage sprigs, for garnish *optional*

SOUP NIGHT MENU

Oak Leaf and Apple Salad with Cider Honey Dressing (**PAGE 121**)
and/or Ham and Cheese Panini with Apple Slaw (**PAGE 141**)

Molasses Spice Cake Squares (**PAGE 167**) *or*
Extra Easy Brown Butter Almond Cake (**PAGE 178**)

"SMOOTH AS SILK"
PARSNIP BISQUE

PREP TIME	START-TO-FINISH	MAKE AHEAD
15 minutes	*45 minutes*	*Yes*

PARSNIPS *are, in my view, under-used and under-appreciated. I love the rustic taste that they impart to soups such as this one, where butter and cream bring out the natural sweetness of this root vegetable. Thyme and bay leaves add an herbal accent, while a hint of wine brightens this extra smooth mélange. When shopping, look for medium-sized parsnips, avoiding the large ones whose woody centers can be bitter.*

IN A HEAVY 4-QUART SAUCEPAN (with a lid) set over medium heat, melt the butter and, when it is hot, add the parsnips and celery. Stir constantly to coat the vegetables with the butter, 3 to 4 minutes until starting to soften. Add the dried thyme, 1 teaspoon salt, and 1/2 teaspoon black pepper. Stir for a few seconds.

ADD THE BROTH, WINE, AND BAY LEAVES. Bring the mixture to a simmer, reduce the heat to low, and cover the pot. Cook until the parsnips are tender, about 20 minutes. Remove and discard the bay leaves.

PURÉE THE SOUP in batches in a food processor, blender, or food mill, then return the soup to the pot. (Or use an immersion blender to purée the soup in the pot.) Whisk in the cream, then the milk. Strain the soup through a fine mesh sieve into a large bowl, pressing down on the solids to extract as much liquid as possible. Taste and season the soup with more salt and pepper if needed. If the soup is too thick, thin with extra broth. (Soup can be prepared one day ahead. Cook to this stage, then cool, cover, and refrigerate. Reheat over medium heat, stirring often.)

TO SERVE, ladle the soup into bowls and garnish each serving with a fresh thyme sprig.

4 TBSP unsalted butter

2 LB parsnips, peeled and cut into 3/4-inch dice

2/3 CUP finely diced celery

1 TSP dried thyme

Kosher salt

Freshly ground black pepper

4 CUPS chicken broth or stock *(or Quick-and-Easy Vegetable Stock, page 200), plus* more if needed

1/4 CUP dry white wine

4 bay leaves, broken in half

2/3 CUP heavy or whipping cream

2 CUPS whole milk

6 fresh thyme sprigs, for garnish

SOUP NIGHT MENU
Winter Greens, Roasted Beets, and Walnuts in Orange Dressing (**PAGE 131**)

Chocolate Cashew Brownies with Chocolate Crème Fraîche Glaze (**PAGE 161**)

CAULIFLOWER SOUP
WITH TOASTED HAZELNUTS & GRUYÈRE

PREP TIME	START-TO-FINISH	MAKE AHEAD
20 minutes	*1 hour*	*Yes*

ON A GRAY, RAINY JANUARY DAY IN PARIS, *I picked up a beautiful cauliflower, some root vegetables, a packet of grated Gruyère, and some hazelnuts at the marché — the makings for a soup to stave off the city's chill. In the tiny kitchen of the apartment my husband and I rent, I sautéed and simmered the vegetables in broth, then puréed the mixture. Instead of the heavy cream I reach for so reflexively when I am in France, I enriched the soup with some milk and guess what? The quartet of vegetables in this recipe provided so much flavor that I didn't miss the taste (or the calories) of the cream at all. As finishing touches, a small sprinkle of Gruyère, a few coarsely chopped hazelnuts, and some snipped chives added color and texture.*

IN A LARGE, HEAVY POT (WITH A LID) over medium heat, heat the oil until hot. Add the leeks, carrots, and celery, and sauté, stirring, until just slightly softened, about 5 minutes. Add the cauliflower florets, stir, and cook 2 minutes more.

ADD 4 CUPS OF BROTH, 1/2 teaspoon salt, cayenne pepper, and several grinds of black pepper. Bring the mixture to a simmer, then reduce the heat to medium low. Cover and cook the soup at a gentle simmer until the vegetables are tender, 20 to 25 minutes or more.

PURÉE THE SOUP in a food processor, blender, or food mill, then return the soup to the pot. (Or use an immersion blender to purée the soup in the pot.) Whisk in 1/2 cup milk. If the soup is too thick, add up to 1 cup or more broth and 1/2 cup additional milk. Season the soup with additional salt if needed. (Soup can be prepared one day ahead. Cook to this stage, then cool, cover, and refrigerate. Reheat over medium heat, stirring often.)

LADLE THE SOUP into bowls. Garnish each serving with a sprinkle of cheese, some toasted hazelnuts, and chives or parsley.

SOUP NIGHT MENU

Radicchio, Spinach, and Red Grapefruit Salad (**PAGE 117**)

Crisp Oatmeal Thins Scented with Orange
served with a bowl of apples or pears (**PAGE 162**)

---

2 TBSP olive oil

1 CUP chopped leeks

1/2 CUP finely diced carrots

1/2 CUP chopped celery

1 HEAD (about 3 lb) of cauliflower, cut to yield 6 cups of florets *(or packaged cauliflower florets)*

4 CUPS chicken broth or stock *(or Quick-and-Easy Vegetable Stock, page 200), plus up to* **1 CUP** or more if needed

Kosher salt

1/8 TSP cayenne pepper

Freshly ground black pepper

1/2 CUP whole milk, *plus* up to **1/2 CUP** more if needed

1/3 CUP grated Gruyère

1/4 CUP coarsely chopped, toasted hazelnuts *see page 202*

1 TBSP chopped chives or flat leaf parsley, for garnish

ROASTED CARROT, PARSNIP & GARLIC SOUP

PREP TIME	START-TO-FINISH	MAKE AHEAD
25 minutes	*1 hour, 30 minutes*	*Yes*

HUMBLE INGREDIENTS—*carrots, parsnips, and garlic—are the foundation of this hearty soup. All are roasted first to bring out their sweetness, then the vegetables are simmered in broth along with leeks until tender. Lastly, a small amount of the cooked vegetables are puréed and stirred back into the pot to thicken this soup. Serve it in the autumn when the weather begins to turn cool, and continue to enjoy warming bowls throughout the cold days of winter.*

ARRANGE A RACK at center position and preheat the oven to 350°F. Have a large rimmed baking sheet ready.

SPREAD THE CARROTS AND PARSNIPS in a single layer on the baking sheet, then arrange the garlic cloves together in a single layer separate from the vegetables on the sheet. Drizzle the vegetables and garlic with the olive oil and toss both with your hands to coat well. Combine 1/2 teaspoon thyme, 1 teaspoon salt, and 1/2 teaspoon black pepper in a small bowl and sprinkle over the vegetables and garlic.

ROAST THE VEGETABLES until the carrots and parsnips are golden brown around the edges and just-tender, and the garlic cloves are softened, 30 to 35 minutes. Stir the vegetables and garlic every 10 minutes while roasting to keep them from sticking to the pan. Remove from the oven when done.

WHEN COOL ENOUGH TO HANDLE, remove the garlic cloves from their skins and set aside.

IN A LARGE, HEAVY POT set over medium heat, melt the butter. Add the leeks and sauté, stirring, until softened, 3 to 4 minutes. Add the roasted carrots and parsnips, stir to coat, and cook about 2 minutes. Stir in the remaining teaspoon of thyme and the broth. Reduce the heat, cover, and cook at a simmer until vegetables are very tender but still hold their shape, 15 to 20 minutes.

REMOVE 3/4 CUP OF THE VEGETABLES and 1/4 cup of the liquid in the pot. Place in a food processor or blender along with the garlic and purée. Whisk it into the soup to thicken it slightly. Season the soup with salt and pepper to taste. (Soup can be prepared one day ahead; cook to this stage, then cool, cover, and refrigerate. Reheat over smedium heat, stirring occasionally.)

LADLE SOUP into bowls and if desired, garnish each serving with a sprig or two of fresh thyme.

1 1/2 LB carrots, peeled and cut into 1/2-inch dice

3/4 LB parsnips, peeled and cut into 1/2-inch dice

10 LARGE
(1/2 – 3/4-inch wide) unpeeled garlic cloves

1/4 CUP olive oil

1 1/2 TSP dried thyme

Kosher salt

Freshly ground black pepper

3 TBSP unsalted butter

2 CUPS (about 3 medium) chopped leeks, white and light green parts only

4 CUPS chicken broth or stock *(or Homemade Vegetable Stock, page 199), plus* more if needed

Several sprigs fresh thyme for garnish *optional*

SOUP NIGHT MENU

Grilled Cheese Tartines (**PAGE 138**) *or* Toasted Baguette
with Smoked Turkey, Prosciutto, Fontina, Garlic Mayo
(**PAGE 147**)

Pumpkin Brownies with Maple Cream Cheese Frosting
(**PAGE 164**)

BROCCOLI SOUP
WITH CURRIED CRÈME FRAÎCHE

PREP TIME	START-TO-FINISH	MAKE AHEAD
15 minutes	*45 minutes*	*Yes*

HERE'S A SOUP *that you can serve any season of the year. It's quick to assemble, takes only 15 minutes to simmer atop the stove, and is light yet totally satisfying. (Buying packaged broccoli florets, rather than slicing them from broccoli crowns saves even more time.) A hint of cayenne pepper adds a bit of heat, but it is the crème fraîche scented with curry powder that is the secret to this dish's vibrant flavor. Some of the cream is swirled into the puréed soup, while the rest is used as a garnish.*

IN A LARGE HEAVY POT (WITH A LID), heat the oil over medium heat. Add the leeks and sauté until softened, about 4 minutes. Add the potato and broccoli florets and sauté, stirring, 1 minute more. Add the chicken broth, 1 teaspoon salt, and 1/8 teaspoon cayenne. Bring to a simmer, cover, and cook until the vegetables are tender, 10 to 15 minutes. Purée the soup in batches in a food processor, blender, or food mill, then return the soup to the pot. (Or use an immersion blender to purée the soup in the pot.)

IN A MEDIUM BOWL, stir together crème fraîche and curry powder. Whisk half of the mixture into the soup until well blended. Taste the soup and season with more salt and additional cayenne pepper if desired. (Soup can be prepared one day ahead; cook to this stage then cool, cover, and refrigerate. Reheat over medium heat, stirring occasionally.)

LADLE soup into bowls and garnish each serving with a dollop of the remaining crème fraîche and a sprinkle of parsley.

3 TBSP olive oil

2 CUPS (2 medium) chopped leeks, white and light green parts only

1 russet potato (about 12-oz), peeled and cut into 1-inch cubes

1 LB broccoli florets

6 CUPS chicken broth or stock *(or Quick-and-Easy Vegetable Stock, page 200)*

Kosher salt

1/8 TSP cayenne pepper, plus more if needed

2/3 CUP crème fraîche *see page 201*

1 TSP curry powder

1 1/2 TBSP chopped flat leaf parsley, for garnish

SOUP NIGHT MENU

Red Leaf and Belgian Endive Salad with Shaved Comté
(PAGE 114)

Chocolate-and-Almond-Studded Shortbread Bars
(PAGE 170)

CREAM OF CELERY ROOT SOUP
WITH CELERY LEAF & HAZELNUT GREMOLATA

PREP TIME	START-TO-FINISH	MAKE AHEAD
20 minutes	*1 hour*	*Yes*

CELERY ROOT, *or celeriac as it is also known, is a vegetable I first tasted when I spent my junior year of college studying in Paris. Most often I ate it in a classic French salad made with grated raw celery root tossed in a mustard mayonnaise, and I still love that dish. But I also loved it cooked and served warm, as it is in this beautiful, creamy soup. The vegetable is diced, then simmered gently in broth with onion and celery before being puréed. A gremolata-style garnish made with chopped celery leaves, parsley, and hazelnuts (instead of the parsley, lemon, and garlic combo called for in the classic Italian topping) adds a pop of color and crunch to this ivory-hued soup.*

IN A LARGE, HEAVY POT over medium heat, melt the butter. When hot, add the celery root, onion, and celery. Sauté the vegetables until slightly softened, stirring often, 3 to 4 minutes. Add the broth, bring the mixture to a simmer, then reduce the heat to medium low. Cover and cook until the vegetables are tender, 20 to 25 minutes.

PURÉE THE SOUP in batches in a food processor, blender, or food mill, and return the soup to the pot. (Or use an immersion blender to purée the soup in the pot.) Return the soup to the pot and stir in 1/2 cup crème fraîche. Taste the soup and season with salt as needed. If the soup is too thick, thin it with a few extra tablespoons of broth. (The soup can be prepared one day ahead. Cook to this stage, then cool, cover, and refrigerate. Reheat over medium heat, stirring often.)

TO PREPARE THE GREMOLATA, in a small bowl combine the celery leaves, hazelnuts, parsley, and lemon zest and mix well. (Gremolata can be prepared 2 hours ahead; cover and refrigerate.)

LADLE THE SOUP into bowls and garnish the center of each with some gremolata and a small dollop of remaining crème fraîche.

MARKET NOTE Celery root has a more concentrated flavor than celery stalks and is available in the produce section of many supermarkets. It has a brown, gnarly exterior and creamy flesh beneath. Use a sharp knife to remove the skin and any dark spots, then dice the flesh. Store it in a plastic bag in the refrigerator.

SOUP NIGHT MENU
Goat Cheese, Radish, and Arugula Panini
(PAGE 143)

Crisp Oatmeal Thins Scented with Orange **(PAGE 162)**
served with a bowl of pears

SOUP

6 TBSP unsalted butter

6 CUPS (from 2 1/2 to 2 3/4 lb celery root) peeled, diced celery root *see Market Note*

1 1/2 CUPS chopped onion

1 1/4 CUPS chopped celery, *plus* celery leaves for the garnish

7 1/2 CUPS chicken broth or stock *(or Quick-and-Easy Vegetable Stock, page 200), plus* more if needed

3/4 CUP crème fraîche, *plus* **3 TBSP** for garnish

Kosher salt

CELERY LEAF & HAZELNUT GREMOLATA

4 TBSP chopped celery leaves

4 TBSP toasted hazelnuts, coarsely chopped *see page 202*

4 TSP chopped flat leaf parsley

1 1/2 TSP grated lemon zest

CALDO VERDE

PREP TIME	START-TO-FINISH	MAKE AHEAD
20 minutes	*1 hour*	*No*

CALDO VERDE *(which translates as "green soup") is a popular soup in Portugal. It is prepared with dark leafy greens like collards, kale, or Swiss chard and with potatoes and sausage. I had tasted several versions in Provincetown, Massachusetts (where the dish arrived long ago with Portuguese immigrants), and had always enjoyed the soup's hearty flavors. My favorite recipe, though, is the following which was shared with me by my Portuguese friend in Paris, Victorine Fernandes.*

IN A LARGE, HEAVY POT over medium heat, heat 3 tablespoons olive oil until hot. Add the onions and sauté until translucent and softened, 3 to 4 minutes. Add the garlic, stir 1 minute more, then add the potatoes and cook, stirring often, for 2 minutes. Add the broth, 1/2 teaspoon salt, and 1/4 teaspoon black pepper. Bring the mixture to a simmer; reduce heat to low, and cook until potatoes are tender, 15 to 20 minutes.

WHILE THE SOUP IS COOKING, prepare the collards. With a sharp knife, remove and discard the tough center stems from each collard leaf. Stack 2 or 3 leaves at a time and cut them crosswise into very thin (1/4 inch) strips. Repeat with remaining leaves. You should have 2 generous cups julienned collards.

IN A MEDIUM SKILLET over medium heat, heat the remaining tablespoon of olive oil. When hot, add the chorizo, and sauté until lightly browned, 2 to 3 minutes. Remove with a slotted spoon and set on paper towels to drain.

WHEN THE SOUP IS DONE, remove the pot from the heat. Using a slotted spoon, transfer 1 cup of the vegetables and 1/4 cup of the liquid from the pot to a food processor or blender. Process for several seconds, pulsing the machine until you have a smooth purée. Stir the purée into the soup to thicken it slightly.

RETURN THE POT TO MEDIUM HEAT and add the collards. Cook until they are just tender and still bright green, about 5 minutes. Stir in 1/2 teaspoon pepper and season with more salt to taste.

LADLE soup into bowls and garnish each serving with some chorizo and a generous drizzle of olive oil.

4 TBSP olive oil, *plus* more for drizzling over the soup

1 1/2 CUPS chopped onion

4 TSP minced garlic

1 1/4 LB Yukon Gold potatoes, peeled and cut into 3/4-inch dice

3 CUPS chicken broth or stock

Kosher salt

Freshly ground black pepper

4 OZ collard greens, rinsed and patted dry

4 OZ chorizo, thinly sliced *(use Spanish-style chorizo in casing, not loose Mexican-style chorizo)*

SOUP NIGHT MENU

Farmers' Market Kale Salad with Pine Nuts and
Golden Raisins (**PAGE 115**)

Extra Easy Brown Butter Almond Cake *served with
vanilla bean ice cream* (**PAGE 178**)

CREAMY ARTICHOKE SOUP
WITH LEMON & TARRAGON

PREP TIME	**START-TO-FINISH**	**MAKE AHEAD**
15 minutes	*50 minutes*	*Partially*

A STUDENT ONCE *described this soup by proclaiming "Artichokes and cream are a match made in heaven!" I couldn't agree more. It is easy and quick to put together and always garners compliments. Frozen artichokes, a real time saver, are simmered in broth along with baby spinach leaves. The latter provides a light-green hue to the soup when it is puréed and enriched with cream. Crisp golden croutons and a sprinkle of fresh tarragon top this silky smooth mélange.*

IN A LARGE, HEAVY POT over medium heat, melt the butter. When hot, add the shallots and sauté, stirring often, until softened, 2 to 3 minutes. Add the dried tarragon and the chopped artichokes and stir 1 minute more. Add the broth and bring the mixture to a simmer.

REDUCE THE HEAT TO LOW and simmer until the artichokes are very tender, 20 to 25 minutes. Stir in the cream. (Soup can be prepared one day ahead; cook to this stage, then cool, cover, and refrigerate. Reheat over medium heat, stirring occasionally.)

ADD THE CHOPPED SPINACH and cook until tender and wilted, 2 to 3 minutes. Purée the soup in a food processor, blender, or food mill, and return the soup to the pot. (Or, use an immersion blender to purée the soup in the pot.) Whisk in the lemon juice and season the soup with salt to taste.

LADLE THE SOUP into bowls. Garnish each serving with some toasted croutons and sprinkle with fresh chopped tarragon. Pass extra croutons in a bowl.

3 TBSP unsalted butter

2/3 CUP chopped shallots

1 TSP dried tarragon

TWO 12-OZ PACKAGES frozen artichokes, defrosted, patted dry, and coarsely chopped

6 CUPS chicken broth or stock (*or Quick-and-Easy Vegetable Stock, page 200*)

1 CUP heavy or whipping cream

2 1/2 CUPS coarsely chopped baby spinach leaves

2 TBSP lemon juice

Kosher salt

Toasted Croutons *see page 201*

2 1/2 TBSP chopped fresh tarragon, for garnish

SOUP NIGHT MENU

Market Salad with Fresh Peas, Radishes, and Melon
(PAGE 127)

Orange Cupcakes with White Chocolate Icing
(PAGE 174)

WINTER TOMATO & GARLIC SOUP
WITH CREAMY GORGONZOLA BRUSCHETTE

PREP TIME	START-TO-FINISH	MAKE AHEAD
15 minutes	*50 minutes*	*Yes*

THIS VIBRANT TOMATO SOUP, *flavored with garlic and an unexpected hint of orange, is a snap to assemble and takes less than half an hour to cook. Canned tomatoes, my go-to option in cold weather, are simmered in stock along with sautéed onions and seasonings of basil and red pepper flakes. Toasted baguette slices topped with Gorgonzola and fresh rosemary can be served alongside or floating on top.*

IN A HEAVY 4-QUART SAUCEPAN over medium heat, heat oil until hot. Add the onions and stir until they start to soften, 3 to 4 minutes. Add the garlic and stir for 1 minute more. Add tomatoes, 3 1/2 cups broth, basil, red pepper flakes, 1/4 teaspoon salt, and sugar. Stir well to combine and bring mixture to a simmer. Reduce heat to low and continue to simmer until vegetables are tender, about 20 minutes.

PURÉE THE SOUP in batches in a food processor, blender, or food mill, then return the soup to the pot. (Or use an immersion blender to purée the soup in the pot.) The mixture will be somewhat chunky. Stir in the half-and-half, Parmesan cheese, and orange zest and cook over medium heat, stirring, until the soup is heated through, 3 to 4 minutes. If the soup is too thick, thin it with 1/2 cup extra broth. Season the soup with salt if needed and, if you'd like more heat, add a pinch of red pepper flakes. (Soup can be prepared two days ahead. Cook to this stage, then cool, cover, and refrigerate. Reheat, stirring often, over medium heat.)

LADLE THE SOUP into bowls. Serve with the Gorgonzola Bruschette alongside or, if you prefer, float one on top of each serving.

3 TBSP olive oil

1 1/2 CUPS chopped onion

2 TBSP minced garlic

TWO 28-OZ CANS diced tomatoes, drained well

3 1/2 CUPS chicken broth or stock *(or Homemade Vegetable Stock, page 199) plus* more if needed

1 TBSP dried basil

SCANT 1/2 TSP red pepper flakes, *plus* more if needed

Kosher salt

2 SMALL PINCHES sugar

3/4 CUP half-and-half

1/4 CUP grated Parmesan cheese, preferably Parmigiano Reggiano

1 TSP grated orange zest

Gorgonzola and Rosemary Bruschette *recipe at left*

GORGONZOLA BRUSCHETTE

12 baguette slices, cut 3/8-inch thick

Olive oil for brushing

ONE 8-OZ piece creamy Gorgonzola, such as Gorgonzola Dolce, softened slightly

1 TBSP chopped fresh rosemary

Arrange a rack at center position and preheat the oven to 350°F. Have a foil-lined baking sheet ready.

Brush both sides of the baguette slices generously with olive oil and place on the baking sheet. Bake slices until golden and just crisp, 3 to 4 minutes per side. *(Slices can be prepared 2 hours ahead. Keep at room temperature.)*

Spread each slice with Gorgonzola, then return to the oven until cheese has melted, 3 to 4 minutes. Sprinkle each slice with chopped rosemary.

> **SOUP NIGHT MENU**
> Arugula and Shaved Fennel Salad in Lemon Dressing
> **(PAGE 135)**
>
> Dark Chocolate Pistachio Brownies with Chocolate
> Glaze **(PAGE 168)** *or* Chocolate Cashew Brownies with
> Chocolate Crème Fraîche Glaze **(PAGE 161)**

BRODO
WITH FRESH PEAS, MINT & PANCETTA

PREP TIME	START-TO-FINISH	MAKE AHEAD
15 minutes	_40 minutes_	_No_

BRODOS (ITALIAN FOR BROTHS) _should always be made with a rich, flavorful base like the one called for here. If you have time, make the broth from scratch (page 196), but if you're rushed, as I usually seem to be, use the delicious Quick-and-Easy version (page 197). Once the broth is simmering, dried orecchiette (a small ear-shaped pasta), fresh peas, snow peas, and chopped Bibb lettuce are stirred into the simmering liquid to cook for a few minutes. Crispy bits of pancetta, fresh mint, and a sprinkling of Parmigiano Reggiano are the simple garnishes._

IN A LARGE, HEAVY POT over medium heat, heat the olive oil until hot. Add the pancetta and cook, stirring, until the pieces are golden and crisp, 3 to 4 minutes. Remove with a slotted spoon and drain on paper towels; set aside for the garnish. Add the leeks to the pot and sauté, stirring, until softened, 2 to 3 minutes. Reduce the heat if the leeks begin to brown too quickly.

ADD THE STOCK and bring the soup to a simmer. Add the pasta and cook 8 minutes, stirring occasionally. Add the fresh peas and snow peas and cook until both are just-tender and the pasta is al dente, 3 to 4 minutes. Stir in the chopped lettuce and cook 1 minute more. Season with salt to taste.

LADLE THE SOUP into shallow bowls and garnish each serving with some mint and pancetta. Place the Parmesan cheese in a small bowl for passing.

MARKET NOTE Orecchiette is available in many supermarkets, but if you can't find it substitute small macaroni or farfalle.

1 TBSP olive oil

1/4 LB finely diced pancetta

1 CUP chopped leeks

8 CUPS Homemade or Quick-and-Easy Chicken Stock _see page 196 or 197_

1 CUP dried orecchiette pasta _see Market Note_

1 LB (3 cups) fresh or defrosted frozen peas

1/4 LB (1 cup) snow peas, trimmed and peas halved on the diagonal

1 CUP Bibb or Boston lettuce, coarsely chopped

Kosher salt

3 TBSP finely julienned mint leaves

1/2 CUP grated Parmesan cheese, preferably Parmigiano Reggiano

SOUP NIGHT MENU
Watercress Salad in an Orange Ginger Dressing
(PAGE 134)

Buttermilk Panna Cottas with Blueberries
(PAGE 186)

BRODO

WITH ASPARAGUS, POTATO GNOCCHI & BLUE CHEESE

PREP TIME
10 minutes

START-TO-FINISH
20 minutes

MAKE AHEAD
Partially

MY HUSBAND AND I *often arrive in Paris in early June when asparagus season is still in full swing and* les primeurs *(produce shops) and grocery stores everywhere proudly display the sleek, long spears. One year, I used this harbinger of spring in an unusual brodo. If you have time, you can make your own broth, but I was pressed and used a high-quality purchased one that I enhanced by simmering with root vegetables. A little blue cheese mixed with some cream whisked into this broth gives it an extra layer of flavor. The asparagus along with gnocchi need only 5 minutes to cook in the robust broth.*

SNAP OFF and discard the tough ends from the asparagus, then cut the spears on the diagonal into 1-inch pieces. Set aside.

IN A SMALL BOWL, use a fork to mash 1/4 cup of the blue cheese with the cream to form a slightly lumpy paste. Set aside.

IN A MEDIUM POT over medium heat, bring the stock to a simmer. Whisk in the blue cheese and cream mixture until it is well blended. In a small bowl combine the cornstarch with 4 teaspoons cold water, then gradually whisk the mixture into the simmering broth. Continue whisking until the broth has thickened slightly, about 3 minutes. Season the broth with salt to taste and add the cayenne pepper. (The stock can be prepared 4 hours ahead; cook to this stage, then cool, cover, and refrigerate. Bring to a simmer over medium heat, stirring, when ready to use.)

ADD THE ASPARAGUS and the gnocchi to the simmering broth and cook until the asparagus are tender and gnocchi have risen to the top of the broth, 3 to 4 minutes. (If the directions on the package of gnocchi call for more than 3 minutes of cooking, add the gnocchi first, then stir in the asparagus during the last 3 minutes of cooking.)

SEASON THE SOUP with more salt and cayenne if needed.

LADLE THE SOUP into bowls and garnish each serving with a sprinkle of green onions and chives, and a few crumbles of remaining blue cheese. (You may have some cheese left over.)

1 LB medium asparagus

5 – 6-OZ wedge blue cheese, such as a creamy Roquefort or St. Augur

1/4 CUP heavy or whipping cream

6 CUPS either Homemade or Quick-and-Easy Chicken Stock *see pages 196 or 197 (or Quick-and-Easy Vegetable Stock, page 200)*

4 TSP cornstarch

Kosher salt

GENEROUS PINCH cayenne pepper

2 CUPS (about 10-oz) purchased potato gnocchi

1/4 CUP chopped green onions, including 1 inch of green stems

2 TBSP chopped chives

> ### SOUP NIGHT MENU
> Romaine, Mint, and Creamy Ricotta Salad
> **(PAGE 119)**
>
> Lemon Pudding "Cakes"
> **(PAGE 180)**

ASPARAGUS BISQUE
with bay scallops, toasted bread
crumbs, and chives

RED PEPPER VELOUTÉ
with crab salad

CREAMY SMOKED TROUT
AND CUCUMBER CHOWDER

MUSSELS IN SAFFRON
TOMATO CRÈME
with garlic toasts

SCALLOP AND FENNEL
CHOWDER *with tarragon*

NEW ENGLAND CORN CHOWDER
with lobster

CORN BISQUE *with pan-seared*
salmon fillets

SEARED SCALLOPS, SHRIMP,
AND COD *in tomato lime broth*

LOUISIANA SEAFOOD GUMBO

VIETNAMESE-STYLE SHRIMP
SOUP *with rice noodles*

BOUILLABAISSE À LA
MARSEILLAISE

2

FISH CHOWDERS, GUMBO, AND BISQUES
FROM THE SEA

BRING A SEAFOOD SOUP to the table and immediately it creates excitement. Seafood transforms itself when simmered in soups— mussels magically open, shrimp turn pink and furl into graceful curves while scallops become a glistening, opaque alabaster. Some soups, such as Provence's bouillabaisse or Vietnamese shrimp soup with noodles, transport us to faraway spots. A steaming bowl of chowder or a soul-satisfying gumbo can also bring back memories of seashores past. In this chapter, you'll see recipes for these soups and many more, all of which pay homage to the bounty of the sea.

Fish soups require planning and some dedicated shopping. You'll need to spend several minutes at the supermarket fish counter, or at the local fishmonger, to select the freshest fish or crustaceans available, and then use your purchases as soon as possible. Once you've taken the time to carefully choose your seafood, however, you'll discover that many fish soups call for a short cooking time and can be whipped up quickly. Seafood often comes with a hefty price tag (one of the reasons people view fish soups as a special indulgence), but the amount of fish called for per serving in most of these soups is less than what you'd need to purchase for individual plated portions.

Popular regional classics such as Bouillabaisse à la Marseillaise and Louisiana Seafood Gumbo appear on the following pages. Both of these coastal specialties are typically assembled with seafood indigenous to the region (think *rascasses* and *rougets* in France, or blue crabs on the Gulf Coast). I've substituted more readily available varieties closer to home, and you can, too.

Chowders, the familiar chunky soups that often include bacon, potatoes, and shellfish, get new variations as well. Scallop and Fennel Chowder with Tarragon and Creamy Smoked Trout and Cucumber Chowder are both refreshing interpretations of a beloved standard. Each has a lighter texture than traditional chowders, for no flour is used to thicken them; whole milk or a touch of cream give these soups all the body they need.

A friend who is a talented cook once confided that she was intimidated when it came to cooking seafood, but not fish soups. She liked the fact that for most she needed only to add fresh seafood to simmering broth or liquids where it would cook in a matter of minutes. Amen to that!

ASPARAGUS BISQUE
with BAY SCALLOPS,
TOASTED BREAD CRUMBS & CHIVES

PREP TIME	START-TO-FINISH	MAKE AHEAD
25 minutes	*1 hour, 10 minutes*	*Partially*

HADLEY, MASSACHUSETTS—*next door to Amherst, where I live—has proudly called itself the asparagus capital of the U.S. since the 1930s. Due to its sandy soil and cool New England climate, Hadley and several surrounding towns produced some of the country's finest stalks. In the 1970s, a fungus took out many of these asparagus crops, but there are still farmers who continue to grow beautiful verdant spears, which in May and June appear in our grocery stores and outdoor markets. This seasonal harvest was the inspiration for a creamy asparagus soup topped with sautéed bay scallops, a sprinkle of chives, and golden breadcrumbs. I like the mildly sweet taste and size of bay scallops, but if you can't find them, sea scallops can be cut into quarters and used in their place.*

IN A LARGE, HEAVY POT over medium heat, melt 3 tablespoons of the butter. When hot, add the leeks and sauté, stirring until softened, 4 to 5 minutes. Add the asparagus and stir and cook 1 minute more.

ADD THE BROTH and bring mixture to a simmer. Reduce the heat to low and cook at a simmer until vegetables are very tender, 15 to 20 minutes. Remove from heat. Purée the mixture in batches in a food processor, blender, or food mill, then return to the pot. (Or use an immersion blender to purée the soup in the pot.)

WHISK IN THE CRÈME FRAÎCHE, lemon juice, and cayenne. Season the bisque with salt to taste. (Soup can be prepared two days ahead. Cook to this stage; cool, cover, and refrigerate. Reheat, stirring, over medium heat.) Return pot to very low heat to keep warm while finishing the soup.

IN A MEDIUM, HEAVY SKILLET over medium-high heat, heat remaining tablespoon of butter and the canola oil. When hot, add scallops, and cook until light golden brown and just cooked through, about 1 to 1 1/2 minutes per side, depending on their size. Season with salt and pepper.

LADLE THE SOUP into shallow soup bowls. Place a few scallops atop each serving, and garnish with a sprinkle of breadcrumbs and chives.

4 TBSP butter

3 CUPS (about 2 large) finely chopped leeks, white and light green parts only

2 LB MEDIUM asparagus, tough ends broken off and discarded and stalks cut into 1-inch pieces

4 CUPS chicken broth or stock

1 CUP crème fraîche *see page 201*

1 1/2 TSP fresh lemon juice

1/8 TSP cayenne pepper

Kosher Salt

1 TBSP canola oil

3/4 LB bay scallops or 10 – 12 medium sea scallops (quartered with side muscles removed and discarded), patted dry

Freshly ground black pepper

1 CUP toasted breadcrumbs *see page 202*

2 TBSP chopped chives

SOUP NIGHT MENU

Goat Cheese, Radish, and Arugula
Panini (**PAGE 143**) *or* Market Salad with Fresh Peas,
Radishes, and Melon (**PAGE 127**)

Orange Cupcakes with White Chocolate Icing
(**PAGE 174**)

RED PEPPER VELOUTÉ
WITH CRAB SALAD

PREP TIME	START-TO-FINISH	MAKE AHEAD
25 minutes	*1 hour, 30 minutes*	*Partially*

ON A WARM SUMMER NIGHT IN PARIS, *my good friend and gifted cook Brigitte Bizot brought out a bright orange soup of puréed red bell peppers. When I asked for the recipe, I was surprised to learn how simple it was. I made it several times, eventually embellishing it with scoops of a refreshing crab salad. The seafood counters the peppers' sweetness with its citrus accent. You can serve this soup warm, at room temperature (as my hostess did), or chilled.*

STEM THE PEPPERS then quarter them lengthwise. Cut out and discard seeds and membranes. Slice peppers lengthwise into 1/2-inch-wide strips to yield about 5 cups.

IN A LARGE, HEAVY POT over low heat, melt butter. When hot, add peppers and stir to coat well with butter, 1 to 2 minutes. Cook, stirring occasionally, until peppers are very soft but not browned, 45 to 50 minutes or more.

ADD BROTH, then whisk in cream cheese. Cook, stirring, until cream cheese has melted and soup is just barely warm, only a few minutes. (Don't worry if there are still specks of cream cheese.)

PURÉE THE SOUP in batches in a food processor or blender, then return it to the pot. (Or, use an immersion blender to purée the soup in the pot.) There may be tiny bits of red pepper remaining after the soup is puréed. If soup is too thick, thin with a few tablespoons of stock or water. Season with salt to taste and a pinch of cayenne for extra heat. (The soup can be prepared one day ahead. Cook to this stage, cool, cover, and refrigerate. Bring to room temperature to serve or reheat if serving warm. If serving chilled, season with more salt if needed since chilled soups often need extra seasoning.)

FOR THE CRAB SALAD, in a medium bowl whisk together mayonnaise, sherry, and orange zest. Stir in crab, green onions, and chives, and mix to blend. (Crab salad can be prepared 4 hours ahead; keep covered and refrigerated.)

TO SERVE, fill a 1/4-cup measuring cup or a small ramekin with crab mixture and unmold in the center of a shallow soup bowl. Ladle some soup around the crab mixture. Repeat to make 5 more servings.

SOUP

1 1/2 LB LARGE (about 6) red bell peppers

4 TBSP unsalted butter

3 CUPS chicken broth or stock, *plus more if needed*

5 OZ cream cheese at room temperature

Kosher salt

PINCH cayenne pepper *optional*

CRAB SALAD

1/2 CUP good-quality (not reduced-fat) mayonnaise

1 1/4 TSP dry sherry

1 TSP grated orange zest

8 OZ fresh crab meat, picked over

3 green onions, including 2 inches of the green stems, chopped

2 1/2 TBSP chopped chives

> **SOUP NIGHT MENU**
>
> Summer Heirloom Tomatos in Crushed Fennel
> Seed Dressing (**PAGE 125**) *or* Romaine, Mint, and Creamy
> Ricotta Salad (**PAGE 119**)
>
> Blueberry Pan Cake with Lemon Crème
> Fraîche (**PAGE 176**) *or* Dark Chocolate Pistachio Brownies
> with Chocolate Glaze (**PAGE 168**)

CREAMY SMOKED TROUT & CUCUMBER CHOWDER

PREP TIME
25 minutes

START-TO-FINISH
1 hour, 30 minutes

MAKE AHEAD
Partially

TWO THINGS CONTRIBUTE *to the appeal of this soup. One is that this chowder (like several others in this chapter) is prepared without flour, resulting in a lighter consistency. The second is that the soup is made with a distinctively flavored fish stock that includes smoked trout, root vegetables, and white wine. Once the stock is prepared, sautéed potatoes and cucumbers along with flakes of smoky trout are stirred in. A touch of cream gives the chowder its soft ivory hue.*

FIRST MAKE THE STOCK. In a large, heavy saucepan or pot combine the leeks, shallots, parsley, wine, crushed black peppercorns, and 4 cups water. Halve one of the trout fillets, leaving the skin intact, and place one portion along with the other fillet in the pot. (Reserve the rest for garnish.) Set the pan over medium heat and bring the mixture to a simmer. Reduce the heat and simmer to develop the flavors, about 15 minutes. Remove the fish fillets with a slotted spoon and, when cool enough to handle, remove and discard the skin and flake the fillets. Set the flaked fish aside to add to the chowder later.

SET A LARGE MESH STRAINER over a large bowl and strain the stock, pressing down with a wooden spoon on all the ingredients to extract as much liquid as possible. You should get 3 cups. Add enough water to make this amount if necessary. (The stock can be prepared two days ahead. Cool, cover, and refrigerate. Wrap the flaked trout and fillet in plastic wrap and refrigerate.)

IN A LARGE, HEAVY POT over medium heat, heat the butter until hot. Add the potatoes and cook, stirring often, until they start browning lightly around the edges, 5 to 7 minutes. Stir in the cucumbers and stir and cook 2 minutes more. Add the stock, 1 teaspoon salt, and 1/4 teaspoon black pepper. Bring to a simmer and cook until the potatoes and cucumbers are very tender, 12 to 15 minutes. Stir in the cream and reserved flaked trout. Season with more salt if needed.

LADLE INTO SOUP BOWLS. Remove the skin from the remaining fish fillet and cut it into thin strips. Garnish each serving with strips of trout, chopped dill, lemon zest, and several grinds of black pepper.

2 CUPS (3 large) coarsely chopped leeks, white and light green parts only

1/2 CUP thickly sliced shallots

2 LARGE parsley sprigs

3/4 CUP dry white wine

1/2 TSP black peppercorns, coarsely crushed

ONE 8-OZ package smoked trout, with two fillets

2 TBSP unsalted butter

1 LB red skin potatoes, peeled and cut into 1/2-inch dice

1 MEDIUM cucumber, peeled, halved lengthwise, seeded, cut into 1/4-inch slices

Kosher salt

Freshly ground black pepper

1/2 CUP heavy or whipping cream

1 TBSP chopped dill

1 1/2 TSP grated lemon zest

SOUP NIGHT MENU

Watercress Salad with Orange-Ginger Dressing
(PAGE 134)

Chocolate-and-Almond-Studded Shortbread Bars
(PAGE 170)

MUSSELS IN SAFFRON TOMATO CRÈME
WITH GARLIC TOASTS

PREP TIME	START-TO-FINISH	MAKE AHEAD
45 minutes	*1 hour, 20 minutes*	*Partially*

I FIRST MADE THIS SOUP *in Paris after visiting* le marché bio, *the city's celebrated organic market, where I bought mussels, summer tomatoes, and other staples for a seafood potage. I quickly cooked the mussels in wine, herbs, and vegetables, then saved the flavorful stock in the pan. It became the base of my soup combined with tomatoes and saffron. At serving time, I added the tender mussels to the creamy broth, leaving a few in their glossy black shells as a garnish.*

TO A 5- TO 6-QUART POT (with a lid), combine mussels, wine, leeks, carrots, and parsley sprigs. Cover and place over medium-high heat. Cook, stirring once or twice, until the mussels open, about 5 minutes. Remove from heat. Discard any unopened ones.

REMOVE MUSSELS FROM THE POT. Strain the cooking liquid and reserve 2 cups. Set aside 8 mussels in their shells for garnish and, when cool enough to handle, remove the remaining mussels from their shells.

IN THE SAME POT over medium heat, heat butter until hot. Add shallots and garlic and cook, stirring just until softened, about 2 minutes. Add the reserved cooking liquid, tomatoes, saffron, and cream. Season soup with 1/2 teaspoon salt, cayenne pepper, and several grinds of black pepper. Reduce heat to low and simmer (do not let mixture come to a boil), 4 to 5 minutes, for flavors to develop. Stir in orange juice. (Soup can be prepared one day ahead. Cook to this stage; cool, cover, and refrigerate. Cover and refrigerate shelled mussels and those in their shells separately. Reheat soup over medium heat.)

ADD SHELLED MUSSELS and cook until heated through, about 2 minutes (slightly longer if they have been refrigerated). Season with additional salt and pepper if needed.

LADLE into shallow bowls. Garnish each serving with 2 mussels in their shells and a sprinkle of parsley. Serve with garlic toasts.

3 LBS mussels, scrubbed, debearded *discard any with open or broken shells*

2 CUPS dry white wine

1 CUP (about 2 medium) finely chopped leeks, white and light green parts only

1/2 CUP sliced carrots

1/2 CUP *plus* **4 TSP** chopped parsley for garnish

4 TBSP unsalted butter

1/3 CUP chopped shallots

2 TSP minced garlic

2 LBS (3 to 4 medium) tomatoes, stemmed, halved, seeded, and diced to make 2 cups

1/8 TSP crushed saffron threads

1/2 CUP whipping or heavy cream

Kosher salt

GENEROUS PINCH cayenne pepper

Freshly ground black pepper

1 1/2 TBSP freshly squeezed orange juice

Garlic Toasts *recipe follows*

GARLIC TOASTS
(MAKES 8 TOASTS)

8 slices crusty country or artisan bread

1 TO 2 peeled garlic cloves

Toast the bread slices and rub generously on one side with a garlic clove.

SOUP NIGHT MENU
Arugula and Shaved Fennel Salad in Lemon Dressing
(PAGE 135)
Extra Easy Brown Butter Almond Cake *with fresh strawberries or blueberries* **(PAGE 178)**

SCALLOP AND FENNEL CHOWDER
WITH TARRAGON

PREP TIME	START-TO-FINISH	MAKE AHEAD
20 minutes	*1 hour, 15 minutes*	*Partially*

A TESTER FOR THIS BOOK *wrote me that she loved this recipe because it is prepared without flour, eliminating the thick and pasty consistency often redolent of seafood chowders. For this variation, pan-seared scallops float in a delicate milk broth studded with bits of fennel, potatoes, and smoky bacon. You can serve this soup any time of the year, but because of its lighter texture, I like to serve it in spring or summer.*

IN A LARGE, HEAVY POT over medium-low heat, sauté the bacon slowly until golden and crisp, about 8 minutes. Remove with a slotted spoon and drain on paper towels. Reserve half of the drippings for sautéing the scallops. To the remaining drippings in the pot, add 4 tablespoons of the butter. When hot, add the fennel and potatoes and sauté, stirring often, until the potatoes are slightly browned around the edges, about 5 minutes.

ADD THE LEEKS and stir 2 minutes. Add the milk, 4 teaspoons tarragon, 1 teaspoon salt, 1/2 teaspoon black pepper, and cayenne pepper. Bring mixture to a simmer, then reduce heat to medium-low. Simmer until the vegetables are tender, about 15 minutes. (Chowder can be prepared one day ahead. Cook to this stage; cool, cover, and refrigerate. Reheat over medium-low heat, stirring often. Transfer the reserved bacon drippings to a small container, cover, and refrigerate.)

PAT THE SCALLOPS DRY with paper towels and season both sides with salt and pepper, and cayenne. In a large, heavy skillet over medium-high heat, heat the reserved bacon drippings and remaining 1 tablespoon butter. When very hot, add the scallops in a single layer and cook until golden, 1 to 2 minutes per side. Repeat using more butter if needed. Remove the scallops to a dinner plate.

TO THE SKILLET, add the wine and mustard and whisk constantly until reduced to about 4 tablespoons. Remove the skillet from the heat and return the scallops and any juices collected on the plate to it. Toss well and add then add the scallops and pan juices to the chowder. Season with salt and pepper if needed.

LADLE INTO SOUP BOWLS and garnish each serving with a sprinkle of tarragon and bacon.

6 THICK BACON SLICES (about 6 oz) cut crosswise into 1/2-inch pieces

5 TBSP unsalted butter, *plus* more if needed

2 CUPS diced fennel

2 CUPS diced russet potato (1/2-inch cubes)

1 1/2 CUPS (about 2 medium) finely chopped leeks, white and light green parts only

5 CUPS whole milk

4 TSP fresh chopped tarragon, *plus* **2 TSP** for garnish

Kosher salt

Freshly ground black pepper

GENEROUS PINCH cayenne pepper

3/4 LB MEDIUM sea scallops, halved horizontally with side muscles removed and discarded

1 CUP dry white wine

2 TSP Dijon mustard

SOUP NIGHT MENU
Romaine, Mint, and Creamy Ricotta Salad
(PAGE 119)

"Melt in Your Mouth" Lemon Rosemary Cookies **(PAGE 172)**
with purchased strawberry sorbet

NEW ENGLAND CORN CHOWDER
WITH LOBSTER

PREP TIME	START-TO-FINISH	MAKE AHEAD
25 minutes	*1 hour, 30 minutes*	*Partially*

TWO STAPLES OF SUMMER COOKING *where I live in Massachusetts are fresh corn and lobster. The latter is typically so plentiful and reasonably priced that you can buy it without having to take out a small loan. In fact, our local groceries will cook lobsters for you, and also sell fresh cooked lobster meat, which I use as the garnish for this New England-inspired chowder. This version is made without potatoes so that corn is the dominant flavor, and is enriched with cream and scented with the smokiness of bacon. It is an indulgent dish—perfect for special occasions.*

PLACE 2 1/2 CUPS OF THE CORN KERNELS and 3/4 cup of the broth in a food processor. Process until it is a thick purée. Set aside.

IN A LARGE, HEAVY POT (with a lid) over medium heat, sauté the bacon until crisp. Remove and drain on paper towels, then chop coarsely. Leave 2 tablespoons of the drippings in the pot and discard the rest. Add the onions and sauté, stirring, until transparent and golden, 3 to 4 minutes.

ADD THE CARROTS, celery, remaining 2 cups corn kernels, 1 teaspoon salt, 1/2 teaspoon black pepper, and cayenne. Stir a minute more. Reduce the heat to low, cover, and cook the vegetables 5 minutes. Add the remaining 3 1/4 cups broth and simmer another 5 minutes. Stir in the corn purée and cream and simmer 5 minutes more.

REMOVE THE POT from the heat and whisk in the sour cream. Season the chowder with more salt and cayenne if needed. (Chowder can be made one day ahead to this stage. Cool, cover, and refrigerate. Reheat over low heat, stirring. Wrap bacon tightly in plastic wrap and refrigerate.)

IN A MEDIUM SKILLET over medium heat, heat the butter until hot. Add the lobster meat and stir just to heat through. Ladle the chowder into bowls and garnish each serving with some lobster meat, bacon, and a sprinkle of chives.

MARKET NOTE If fresh cooked lobster meat is available at your local grocery or fish market, you'll find it costs more than whole lobsters, but is a great time saver. You can also cook lobsters yourself. A pound of uncooked lobster will yield about 1/4 pound cooked meat. For this recipe you'll need to cook 3 pounds of lobster to get 12 ounces of cooked meat.

4 1/2 CUPS (scraped from 5 – 6 ears) fresh corn kernels

4 CUPS chicken broth or stock

5 SLICES (4 to 5-oz) bacon

1 CUP chopped onion

1/2 CUP finely diced carrots

1/2 CUP finely diced celery

Kosher salt

Freshly ground black pepper

1/8 TSP cayenne pepper, *plus* more if needed

1 CUP heavy or whipping cream

1/4 CUP sour cream

4 TSP unsalted butter

12 OZ cooked lobster meat, cut into generous bite-size pieces *see Market Note*

2 TBSP chopped chives

SOUP NIGHT MENU

Summer Heirloom Tomatoes in Crushed Fennel
Seed Dressing (**PAGE 125**)

Lime and Ginger Cream Cheese Bars
(**PAGE 157**)

CORN BISQUE
WITH PAN-SEARED SALMON FILLETS

PREP TIME	START-TO-FINISH	MAKE AHEAD
20 minutes	*1 hour, 30 minutes*	*Partially*

SEVERAL YEARS AGO *at a charming restaurant called The Lumber Yard in Amherst, Massachusetts, I ordered their corn chowder, which came topped with a thin fillet of pan-seared salmon. I loved the combination and thought about the dish every time the corn season arrived. Finally, I worked out my own version. Instead of creating a chowder, in which all the ingredients float in a broth, I decided on a smooth, puréed corn bisque. Then I stirred some sautéed corn into the soup, and topped each bowl with a seared, spice-rubbed salmon fillet.*

IN A LARGE, HEAVY POT (with a lid) over medium-high heat, heat 3 tablespoons butter. When hot, add onion, carrots, and celery and sauté, stirring, 3 minutes. Add 4 cups of the corn, rosemary, and cayenne pepper. Cook, stirring, 2 minutes. Add the broth and bring the mixture to a simmer. Reduce heat to low and simmer, with the lid set slightly ajar, until vegetables are tender, 25 to 30 minutes.

PURÉE THE SOUP in batches until it is very smooth in a food processor, blender, or food mill, and return it to the pot. (Or use an immersion blender to purée the soup in the pot.) Stir in the half-and-half. Set a large mesh strainer over a large bowl and strain the soup in batches. Pressing down with a rubber spatula on the solids to release as much liquid as possible. Be sure to scrape the puréed mixture from the bottom of the strainer. You should get 5 cups. Discard any solids left in the strainer and return the soup to the pot.

IN A MEDIUM, HEAVY SKILLET over medium heat, melt remaining 1 1/2 tablespoons butter. When hot, add the remaining corn kernels and cook, stirring occasionally, until the corn takes on a little color, 4 to 5 minutes. Season the corn with salt and pepper; then stir into the bisque. Season the soup with salt and pepper. (Soup can be prepared one day ahead. Cook to this stage; cool, cover, and refrigerate. Reheat over medium heat, stirring.)

LADLE THE BISQUE into shallow soup bowls. Garnish each serving with a sautéed salmon fillet and a sprinkle of chives.

4 1/2 TBSP unsalted butter

1 1/2 CUPS chopped onion

3/4 CUP diced carrots

3/4 CUP diced celery

5 1/2 CUPS (from 6 – 7 ears) fresh corn kernels

3/4 TSP crushed dried rosemary *see page 203*

GENEROUS 1/8 TSP cayenne pepper

3 CUPS chicken broth or stock

3/4 CUP half-and-half

Kosher salt

Freshly ground black pepper

Seared Salmon Fillets *recipe follows*

1 TBSP chopped chives

SOUP NIGHT MENU

Romaine, Avocado, Tomato, and Queso Fresco
in Cumin Lime Dressing **(PAGE 122)**

Cherries Poached in Red Wine and Spices
(PAGE 182)

SEARED SALMON FILLETS

ONE 10-OZ salmon fillet, about 1-inch thick, with skin removed

1 TSP mild smoked paprika
see page 203

SCANT 1/2 TSP kosher salt

1/2 TSP dried thyme

1/2 TSP crushed dried rosemary

1/4 TSP freshly ground black pepper

1 TBSP unsalted butter

1 TBSP canola oil

Holding a sharp knife parallel to the work surface, halve the salmon fillet horizontally to make 2 thinner fillets. Halve those in half vertically to make 4 pieces. (Or, ask your fishmonger to cut an evenly thick fillet near the tail, and slice it into 4 pieces as described.)

In a small bowl, mix together smoked paprika, salt, thyme, rosemary, and pepper and rub each salmon slice on both sides with the seasoning.

In a medium, heavy skillet over medium-high heat, heat the butter and canola oil until very hot. Add the salmon and cook 1 to 2 minutes per side until lightly browned.

SEARED SCALLOPS, SHRIMP & COD IN TOMATO LIME BROTH

PREP TIME
45 minutes

START-TO-FINISH
1 hour, 40 minutes

MAKE AHEAD
Partially

THIS SOUP IS SIMILAR TO CIOPPINO, *a fish stew that is a specialty of San Francisco. In cioppino, fresh fish and shellfish are surrounded by a spicy, Italian-scented tomato broth. For this version, Spanish and Mexican seasonings flavor a light lime-accented tomato soup studded with corn and red bell peppers. It is ladled over a glorious sauté of scallops, shrimp, and cod.*

IN A LARGE, HEAVY POT over medium heat, heat 2 tablespoons oil until hot. Add the peppers, leeks, and corn. Cook, stirring until softened, about 10 minutes. Add the garlic, 1 teaspoon paprika, and 1/2 teaspoon salt. Stir 1 minute more.

ADD THE RED PEPPER FLAKES, bay leaves, tomatoes, broth, 1/4 cup lime juice, and cilantro. Bring the mixture to a simmer. Reduce the heat to low and cook for flavors to meld, 20 minutes. Remove and discard the bay leaves. (Soup can be prepared one day ahead. Cook to this stage; cool, cover, and refrigerate. Reheat over medium heat.)

IN A SMALL BOWL, stir together remaining 1/2 teaspoon smoked paprika and 1/2 teaspoon each salt and pepper. Pat scallops, shrimp, and cod dry with paper towels, then season them with paprika mixture. In a large, heavy skillet over medium-high heat, heat remaining 2 tablespoons oil until hot. Add the seafood and cook, stirring often, until the shrimp are curled and pink and scallops and cod are opaque, 2 to 3 minutes or more. Season with salt and pepper and, if desired, an extra pinch of red pepper flakes.

DIVIDE THE SEAFOOD among shallow soup bowls and ladle some of the hot tomato broth over each serving. Whisk together remaining 1 1/2 tablespoons olive oil and 1 1/2 teaspoons lime juice. Garnish each serving with a drizzle of lime oil and a sprig of cilantro.

5 1/2 TBSP olive oil, *plus* **1 1/2 TBSP** more for garnish

1 MEDIUM red bell pepper, seeds and membranes removed, cut into 1/8-inch wide by 2-inches long strips

1 CUP (about 2 medium) finely chopped leeks, white and light green parts only

1 CUP (about 2 ears) fresh corn kernels

1 1/2 TBSP minced garlic

1 1/2 TSP smoked paprika *see page 203*

Kosher salt

1/4 TSP red pepper flakes, *plus* more if needed

2 bay leaves, broken in half

ONE 28-OZ CAN diced tomatoes, drained

4 CUPS chicken broth or stock

1/4 CUP *plus* **1 1/2 TSP** lime juice

1/4 CUP chopped cilantro, *plus* sprigs for garnish

Freshly ground black pepper

1/2 LB bay scallops, or medium sea scallops, halved horizontally with side muscles removed

1/2 LB (30 count) large shrimp, peeled and deveined

3/4 LB cod fillet, about 1-inch thick, cut into 1-inch cubes

SOUP NIGHT MENU

Arugula and Shaved Fennel Salad in Lemon Dressing
(PAGE 135)

Extra Easy Brown Butter Almond Cake *with fresh strawberries or blueberries* **(PAGE 178)**

LOUISIANA SEAFOOD GUMBO

PREP TIME	START-TO-FINISH	MAKE AHEAD
40 minutes	*1 hour, 45 minutes*	*Partially*

I REMEMBER SPENDING LONG AFTERNOONS *as a youngster crabbing on the Gulf Coast with my aunt, uncle, and cousins. When our haul was complete, we'd return to their home where my aunt would make a rich seafood gumbo. I live in Massachusetts now, where those blue crabs I remember from long ago are not anywhere to be found, but that hasn't stopped me from making Louisiana-style gumbos. I use shrimp and scallops, both readily available in local groceries. My version is also prepared with a quick roux that takes far less time than the traditional method and, instead of simmering okra in the pot, I sauté it in hot oil which keeps it from becoming stringy. Serve the gumbo piping hot over rice.*

FOR THE ROUX, in a medium, heavy skillet (cast iron works particularly well) over medium-low heat, heat 4 tablespoons oil until hot. Add the flour and stir constantly with a wooden spoon until the mixture thickens and turns a rich deep brown color, 6 to 8 minutes. Watch carefully so that the roux does not burn. Remove from the heat and, immediately, carefully, transfer the roux to a heatproof bowl.

FOR THE GUMBO, in a large, deep pot over medium heat, heat 1 tablespoon of oil. Add the sausage and cook, stirring often, until lightly browned, 4 to 5 minutes. Remove with a slotted spoon and drain on paper towels. Do not discard the drippings in the pan. You should have about 2 tablespoons. If not, add enough oil to make this amount and heat until hot.

ADD THE ONION, celery, red and yellow peppers, and garlic. Cook, stirring, until softened, about 5 minutes. Stir in thyme, 1 teaspoon salt, cayenne, tomatoes, clam juice, 1 1/2 cups water, and wine. Add bay leaves and parsley sprigs. Bring the mixture to a simmer, then whisk in the roux until it is blended well.

REDUCE THE HEAT TO LOW AND COOK the gumbo at a simmer until the vegetables are tender, 15 to 20 minutes. Remove and discard the bay leaves and parsley sprigs.

IN A LARGE, HEAVY SKILLET over medium-high heat, heat the 2 remaining tablespoons of oil until hot. Add the okra and cook, stirring often, until lightly browned, 4 to 5 minutes. Season with salt, then add to the pot of cooked vegetables along with the sausage. (Gumbo can be prepared one day ahead. Cook to this stage; then cool, cover, and refrigerate. Reheat over medium heat.)

CONTINUED ⇀

ROUX

4 TBSP canola or vegetable oil

4 TBSP all-purpose flour

GUMBO

3 TBSP canola or vegetable oil, *plus* more if needed

6 OZ andouille sausage, cut into 1/2-inch dice

1 CUP chopped onion

3/4 CUP diced celery

1/2 CUP diced red bell pepper

1/2 CUP diced yellow bell pepper

2 1/2 TSP minced garlic

1 1/2 TSP dried thyme

1/4 TSP cayenne pepper, *plus* more if needed

Kosher salt

ONE 15-OZ CAN diced tomatoes, drained well

3 CUPS clam juice

ADD THE SHRIMP and scallops to the pot. Cook until the shrimp are curled and pink and the scallops are opaque, 3 to 4 minutes. Season the gumbo with salt, several grinds of black pepper, and, if desired, with more cayenne.

MOUND 1/2 CUP OF RICE into soup bowls. Ladle gumbo over each serving.

SOUP NIGHT MENU

Toasted Baguette, Smoked Turkey, Fontina,
and Garlic Mayo **(PAGE 147)** *or*
Arugula and Shaved Fennel Salad in Lemon Dressing
(PAGE 135)

Three-Layer Chocolate Caramel Bars
(PAGE 159)

1/2 CUP dry white wine

2 bay leaves,
broken in half

4 parsley sprigs

2 CUPS fresh or frozen
okra (defrosted and
patted dry), sliced 1/4-
inch thick

1/2 LB (30 count) large
shelled and deveined
shrimp, uncooked

1/2 LB medium sea
scallops, side muscles
removed and discarded,
halved horizontally

Freshly ground
black pepper

3 CUPS cooked
long-grain white rice

VIETNAMESE-STYLE SHRIMP SOUP
WITH RICE NOODLES

PREP TIME	START-TO-FINISH	MAKE AHEAD
35 minutes	*1 hour, 20 minutes*	*No*

THIS SOUP DRAWS ON THE FLAVORS *of Southeast Asia with accents of lemongrass, ginger, and fish sauce used in the flavorful broth. Count on several minutes to chop the vegetables and herbs, but once that's is done, the rest goes quickly. The broth needs only 10 minutes to simmer, and the shrimp and vegetables require less time than that to cook in it. Ladled over rice noodles, this brightly colored soup is good any time of the year.*

PREPARE THE RICE NOODLES according to package directions. Drain and set aside.

IN A LARGE, HEAVY POT (with a lid) over medium heat, add broth, lemongrass, fish sauce, garlic, ginger, and red pepper flakes. Stir to blend, then cover. Simmer to develop the flavors, 10 minutes. Strain the mixture, pressing down on the solids to extract as much liquid as possible. You should have 6 cups; if not, add more broth to make this amount. Return strained mixture to the same pot over medium heat.

ADD RED BELL PEPPER strips and cook 5 minutes. Season shrimp with salt and pepper, add them to the pot, and cook only 1 minute. Remove pan from heat and add spinach and 1/2 cup of the cilantro. Let stand, stirring once or twice, until spinach and cilantro have wilted, about 2 minutes.

DIVIDE THE NOODLES and green onions among bowls and ladle soup over them. Garnish each serving with a lime wedge. Serve with the remaining chopped cilantro on the side and, if desired, sliced jalapenos. You can include chop sticks along with spoons when serving this soup.

MARKET NOTE You can find brown rice noodles in the Asian section of many supermarkets and in Asian grocery stores. I like the elegant look of these long noodles, but feel free to break them in half so they are easier to eat with a spoon.

4 OZ brown rice noodles *see Market Note*

6 CUPS chicken broth or stock, *plus* more if needed

1/2 CUP (about 5 stalks) thinly sliced lemongrass *see page 203*

1 TBSP fish sauce

3 MEDIUM garlic cloves, smashed and peeled

FOUR 1/4-inch-thick rounds of ginger, peeled and smashed

SCANT 1/2 TSP red pepper flakes

1 large red bell pepper, seeds and membranes removed, cut into strips 1/4 inch wide by 2-inches long

Kosher salt

Freshly ground black pepper

1 LB (30 count) large shrimp, shelled and deveined

1 1/2 CUPS baby spinach leaves

3/4 CUP chopped cilantro

4 – 6 green onions, including 4 inches of the green stems, cut thinly on a sharp diagonal, to yield 1 cup

6 lime wedges, for garnish

1 small jalapeno pepper with seeds, sliced very thinly, for garnish *optional*

SOUP NIGHT MENU

Shredded Romaine and Cucumbers with Lime Dressing
(PAGE 132)

Crisp Oatmeal Thins Scented with Orange **(PAGE 162)**
with a bowl of diced fresh mango

BOUILLABAISSE À LA MARSEILLAISE

PREP TIME
40 minutes

START-TO-FINISH
1 hour, 25 minutes

MAKE AHEAD
Partially

WHEN A FRENCH FRIEND *in my small New England town learned that I was working on a recipe for bouillabaisse, she immediately asked, "but what about les petits poissons?" She was referring to the small Mediterranean fish used to make this chowder in the south of France. "I'm replacing them with our local varieties," I enthusiastically replied. On this side of the Atlantic, I've discovered that a mix of firm white fish such as cod, monkfish, or haddock works beautifully when combined with shellfish like mussels and shrimp. They are cooked quickly in a fish stock seasoned with saffron and anise-scented Pernod. But no matter where it's prepared, no bouillabaisse would be complete without rouille (a rust-hued garlic and red bell pepper purée) and toasted bread slices. Both take only minutes to prepare.*

FOR THE BOUILLABAISSE, in a large, heavy pot (with a lid) over medium heat, heat the olive oil until hot. Add the leeks, fennel, and garlic and cook, stirring constantly, until leeks are just translucent, 3 to 4 minutes.

ADD TOMATOES, fish stock, wine, saffron, 1/2 teaspoon salt, and orange peel. Bring to a simmer. Reduce heat and simmer 25 minutes. Remove and discard the orange peel. The soup will have the consistency of a light broth and will not be thick. Season with more salt if needed. (Bouillabaisse can be prepared one day ahead. Cook to this stage; cool cover, and refrigerate. Reheat over medium heat, stirring occasionally.)

TURN THE HEAT TO MEDIUM, and add the cubed fish, mussels, shrimp, and Pernod. Cover and cook until mussels have opened, shrimp are curled and pink, and fish cubes are opaque, 4 to 5 minutes. (Discard any mussels that have not opened.) Season with salt if needed.

LADLE INTO SHALLOW BOWLS. Garnish each serving with a sprinkle of parsley. Serve with a basket of toasted baguette slices and a bowl of rouille for spreading on them.

3 TBSP olive oil

1 1/4 CUPS (2 medium) finely chopped leeks, white and light green parts only

1 CUP chopped fennel

2 TSP chopped garlic

ONE 14.5-OZ CAN diced tomatoes, drained well

6 CUPS Quick-and-Easy Fish Stock *see page 200*

3/4 CUP dry white wine

SCANT 1/4 TSP saffron threads, crushed

Kosher salt

ONE 4-BY-1-INCH fresh orange peel

1 1/4 LBS firm white fish fillets, such as cod, monkfish, or haddock, cut into 1-inch cubes

3/4 LB mussels, scrubbed and debearded *discard any that are open or with broken shells*

3/4 LB MEDIUM – LARGE shrimp (30 count) shelled and deveined

1 – 1 1/2 TBSP Pernod (a liqueur available in wine and spirits stores)

1 TBSP chopped flat leaf parsley

Rouille *recipe follows*

Toasted baguette slices *recipe follows*

> ### SOUP NIGHT MENU
> Arugula and Shaved Fennel Salad in Lemon Dressing
> **(PAGE 135)**
>
> Rustic Apricot Tart **(PAGE 184)**

CONTINUED →

ROUILLE
(MAKES ABOUT 3/4 CUP)

1 TBSP chopped garlic

1/4 TSP sea salt, such as
fleur de sel, or kosher salt

3/4 CUP toasted bread crumbs
see page 202

1/2 CUP chopped jarred
roasted red peppers

1/3 CUP olive oil

PLACE THE GARLIC and the salt in a mortar and smash with a
pestle, or place in a small bowl and smash with a fork. Transfer to
a food processor.

ADD THE BREAD crumbs and roasted red pepper to the processor
and pulse several times to chop coarsely. Stop the machine and
pour in the olive oil. Process until mixture is well blended and
smooth, about 1 minute. (Rouille can be made 4 hours ahead; cover
and refrigerate.)

TOASTED BAGUETTE SLICES
(MAKES 18 TOASTS)

1 baguette, cut into 18 slices
1/4-inch-thick

Olive oil for brushing

ARRANGE A RACK at center of oven and preheat the oven to 350°F.
Place the bread slices on a baking sheet and brush on both sides
with olive oil. Bake until slices are crisp and golden, 4 to 5 minutes
per side. Remove and, if not using immediately, leave at room
temperature uncovered for up to 1 hour.

WINTER VEGETABLE AND
BARLEY SOUP

EMILY'S BEANS AND GREENS
SOUP *over mounds of brown rice*

BLACK BEAN SOUP *with
lime-pickled red onions*

FENNEL AND WHITE BEAN SOUP
*with crispy prosciutto and golden
croutons*

TOMATO AND CHICKPEA SOUP
with yogurt and mint

FENNEL AND CARROT BRODO
over red quinoa

NEW ORLEANS RED BEANS
AND RICE SOUP *with scallion-bacon
garnish*

HARIRA (MOROCCAN LENTIL,
CHICKPEA, AND LAMB SOUP)

SPICY RED LENTIL SOUP *with
butternut squash and cauliflower*

COLORADO CHICKEN SOUP
with black beans, corn, and pepitas

3

·····················

NEW AND CLASSIC
BEAN AND GRAIN SOUPS

BY NOW, EVERYONE KNOWS the healthy benefits of beans and grains, whether they be familiar staples like dried or canned beans that line our grocery shelves so abundantly or those "new" ancient grains like quinoa or farro. But nutritional merits are not why I love to use these ingredients in soups. It's the color, texture, and flavor that beans and grains impart to simmering broths that I find enticing. Many beloved soup recipes from around the world already include them—robust bean soups from Italy, spicy black bean ones from Mexico, and Moroccan specialties that include chickpeas come to mind.

Along with reaching for packages of beans and grains to cook such classics, I am always searching for new, imaginative ways to use them in soups. You'll discover a mix of both on the pages that follow. There are traditional bean or grain soups with fresh twists as well as some of my more recent creations. All share the advantages, though, of being economical and uncomplicated to prepare.

The warming soups in this chapter include beans and grains of varying colors and shapes. You'll find red and black beans, cannellini beans, and lentils (both coral and green), plus black-eyed peas and green-hued pigeon peas bobbing in various flavorful broths. Beautiful red quinoa delivers a textural and visual pop to a carrot and fennel brodo. Pearl barley partners with winter vegetables, including butternut squash and collards in another hearty combination. Nutritional powerhouses, such as collards and kale pair well with beans and grains, and make appearances in many of these recipes, too.

Several of these soups like Spicy Red Lentil Soup with Butternut Squash and Cauliflower and a delicious Tomato and Chickpea Soup with Yogurt and Mint are vegetarian when prepared with one of the vegetable stocks from the Basics section of this book. In others, meat is used as an accent, not the main focus. Crispy sautéed prosciutto garnishes an earthy fennel and white bean dish, while a touch of lamb imparts its robust flavor to a classic Moroccan lentil and chickpea soup known as harira.

When making bean and grain soups in advance, keep in mind that these ingredients often absorb some of the liquid surrounding them as they rest, resulting in thicker consistencies. It's a good idea, then, to have extra stock on hand for thinning when preparing these soups.

Inexpensive, easy to store, and packed with flavor, beans and grains have long been the pantry darlings of home cooks. The recipes in this chapter will give you even more delicious reasons to keep them on hand.

WINTER VEGETABLE & BARLEY SOUP

PREP TIME	START-TO-FINISH	MAKE AHEAD
40 minutes	*1 hour, 25 minutes*	*Partially*

UNLIKE TRADITIONAL BEEF AND BARLEY SOUP, *this lighter version showcases hearty, cold-weather vegetables that are cooked with pearl barley and a small amount of smoked ham. What adds immeasurably to this dish's flavor, though, is a simple herb purée prepared with fresh rosemary, parsley, and sage that gets stirred in during the last few minutes of simmering.*

IN A HEAVY, LARGE POT over medium heat, heat 1 tablespoon of the oil until hot. Add ham and cook, stirring, until it starts to brown lightly around the edges, 2 to 3 minutes. Remove with a slotted spoon and drain on paper towels.

TO THE SAME POT, add 2 more tablespoons of olive oil. When hot, add the leeks and fennel and cook, stirring constantly, 3 minutes. Add 4 cups chicken broth and 1/4 teaspoon salt. Bring the mixture to a simmer. Reduce the heat to low and add the butternut squash and the barley. Cover and cook 20 minutes.

MEANWHILE, prepare the herb mixture. In a food processor or blender, place the garlic, crushed fennel seeds, parsley, rosemary, sage, red pepper flakes, 1 1/2 teaspoons lemon zest, and 1 tablespoon of olive oil. Pulse the mixture several times until it is a coarse purée.

STIR IN THE HERB MIXTURE and the reserved ham. (Soup can be prepared one day ahead. Cook to this stage, then cool, cover, and refrigerate. Reheat over medium heat.)

JUST BEFORE SERVING, add the collards to the pot and cook until the greens are tender and still bright green, 10 minutes or more. If the soup is too thick, thin with 1 to 2 cups extra broth. Season the soup with more salt, red pepper flakes, and up to 1/2 teaspoon lemon zest if needed.

LADLE SOUP INTO BOWLS. Garnish each serving with several grinds of black pepper. If you like, pass a bowl of Parmesan cheese for sprinkling.

4 TBSP olive oil

1 CUP (6-oz) finely diced smoked ham

1 CUP (about 2 medium) finely chopped leeks, white and light green parts only

1 1/2 CUPS finely diced fennel

4 CUPS chicken broth or stock, *plus* up to **2 CUPS** more if needed

Kosher salt

1 1/2 CUPS butternut squash, cut into 1/2-inch cubes *(or purchase same quantity of pre-cut squash)*

1/3 CUP pearl barley

2 TSP chopped garlic

1 TSP fennel seeds, crushed *see page 203*

2 TBSP chopped flat leaf parsley

1 1/2 TBSP chopped rosemary

1 TBSP chopped sage

1/8 TSP red pepper flakes, *plus* more if needed

1 1/2 – 2 TSP grated lemon zest

2 CUPS (4 to 5-oz) packed coarsely chopped collard greens, with tough ribs removed and discarded

Freshly ground black pepper

1/2 CUP grated Parmesan cheese, preferably Parmigiano Reggiano *optional*

> ### SOUP NIGHT MENU
>
> Chicken Salad with Fennel and Walnuts on Whole Wheat (**PAGE 153**) *or* Arugula and Shaved Fennel Salad in Lemon Dressing (**PAGE 135**)
>
> Butterscotch Pots de Crème (**PAGE 189**)

EMILY'S BEANS & GREENS SOUP
OVER MOUNDS OF BROWN RICE

PREP TIME	START-TO-FINISH	MAKE AHEAD
30 minutes	*1 hour, 30 minutes*	*Yes*

A FEW YEARS AGO *while visiting my assistant Emily Bell in Ohio, I fell hard for a soup she served. On a chilly fall night, she placed a shallow bowl in front of me with a mound of brown rice in the center and a beautiful rust-hued broth with chopped greens and beans ladled over it. Her mélange included smoked meat, root vegetables, and herbs. However, it was the collards and kale combined with the black-eyed peas and field peas that gave this soup its distinctive flavor. In this version, green pigeon peas stand in for field peas with equally tempting results.*

IN A LARGE DEEP-SIDED POT over medium heat, heat 2 tablespoons of the olive oil. When hot, add ham and sauté, stirring until lightly browned, 3 to 4 minutes. With a slotted spoon, remove and drain on paper towels.

TO THE SAME POT add remaining tablespoon oil and onion, carrots, celery, thyme, and rosemary. Stir constantly until vegetables start to soften and are lightly browned, 6 to 8 minutes. Add potato and garlic and stir 2 minutes. Add half of the collards and of the kale and cook, stirring, until the greens are almost wilted. Add remaining greens and the ham and stir until the greens have wilted, 2 to 3 minutes.

ADD TOMATOES with their juices, 6 cups of the chicken broth, black-eyed peas, and pigeon peas. Bring to a simmer, reduce heat and simmer, uncovered, until greens are tender and soup has thickened, 35 to 40 minutes. If soup is too thick, thin with up to 2 cups of remaining broth. Season with salt and pepper. (Soup can be prepared two days ahead. Cook to this stage; cool, cover, and refrigerate. Reheat over medium heat, stirring occasionally, and thinning with additional broth or water if needed.)

PLACE MOUNDS OF cooked brown rice in the center of shallow soup bowls. Ladle soup over each serving, and if you like, garnish with a pinch of red pepper flakes.

3 TBSP olive oil

3/4 CUP (4 – 5-oz) finely diced smoked ham

1 1/2 CUPS chopped onion

3/4 CUP finely diced carrots

3/4 CUP finely diced celery

1 TBSP dried thyme

1 TBSP crushed dried rosemary *see page 203*

ONE 8-OZ Yukon Gold potato, finely diced

1 TBSP minced garlic

8 OZ collard greens, stems and center veins removed, leaves chopped

8 OZ kale, stems and center veins removed, leaves chopped

ONE 28-OZ CAN diced tomatoes, with their juices

6 – 8 CUPS chicken broth or stock, *plus* more if needed

ONE 15-OZ CAN black-eyed peas, drained and rinsed, or 1 1/2 cups frozen peas, defrosted

ONE 15-OZ CAN green pigeon peas, drained and rinsed *see Market Note*

Kosher salt

Freshly ground black pepper

4 CUPS cooked brown rice

Red pepper flakes *optional*

MARKET NOTE Pigeon peas are light green, rounded peas used in Caribbean cooking. They are often located in the supermarket aisle with Latin American ingredients. Southern field peas can be substituted.

SOUP NIGHT MENU

Arugula and Shaved Fennel Salad in Lemon Dressing
(PAGE 135)

Chocolate-and-Almond-Studded
Shortbread Bars **(PAGE 170)**
and a bowl of Clementines or tangerines.

BLACK BEAN SOUP
WITH LIME-PICKLED RED ONIONS

PREP TIME	START-TO-FINISH	MAKE AHEAD
20 minutes	1 hour, 20 minutes	Partially

HERE'S A HEARTY BEAN SOUP *that stands on its own without the addition of any meat. A generous mix of spices, including an unexpected hint of sweetness from cinnamon sticks, punches up the flavor, but it's the garnish that makes this dish memorable. Crunchy lime-pickled red onions paired with avocado cubes float atop each serving.*

IN A LARGE, HEAVY POT over medium heat, heat the oil until hot. Add the onion and celery and cook, stirring often, 4 minutes. Add the garlic and stir 1 minute more. Stir in the cumin, oregano, 3/8 teaspoon chipotle chili powder, and 1/2 teaspoon salt and stir 1 minute more. Add the black beans, chicken broth or vegetable stock, and cinnamon sticks.

BRING THE MIXTURE TO A SIMMER. Reduce the heat to low, and simmer until the soup has reduced by about a third (to about 8 cups) and has thickened, 40 to 45 minutes. Season the soup with salt to taste, and with 1/8 teaspoon chipotle chili powder if you'd like more heat. Remove and discard the cinnamon sticks. (Soup can be prepared one day ahead. Cook to this stage; cool, cover, and refrigerate. Reheat over medium heat, stirring often. If the soup is too thick, thin with more broth.)

FOR THE LIME-PICKLED RED ONIONS, peel, then halve the onion through the root end. Cut each half crosswise into very thin slices to yield 1 1/2 cups. Transfer onions to a medium nonreactive bowl and toss well with the lime juice, salt, sugar, and 1 tablespoon cilantro. Marinate onions for 30 minutes; they will still be crisp. (Onions can be prepared 2 hours ahead. Keep covered and refrigerated. Bring to room temperature 30 minutes before using.)

LADLE soup into bowls. Garnish each serving with pickled onions (spooning a little of the marinating liquids along with them), diced avocado and a sprinkle of cilantro. Pass extra onions in a bowl.

SOUP

3 TBSP olive oil

2 CUPS chopped onion

3/4 CUP diced celery

2 1/2 TSP finely chopped garlic

2 1/2 TSP ground cumin

1 1/4 TSP oregano

3/8 TSP chipotle chili powder *plus more for a spicier taste*

Kosher salt

4 15-OZ CANS black beans, rinsed well and drained

5 CUPS chicken broth or stock *(or Homemade Vegetable Stock page 199), plus* more if needed

2 cinnamon sticks, broken in half

LIME-PICKLED RED ONIONS AND AVOCADO GARNISH

1 large red onion

1/4 CUP lime juice

Kosher salt

1/2 TSP sugar

1 TBSP chopped cilantro, *plus* **2 TSP** more for garnish

2 ripe avocados, cut into 1/2-inch cubes

SOUP NIGHT MENU

Romaine, Avocado, Tomato, and Queso Fresco in Cumin Lime Dressing (**PAGE 122**)

Chocolate Cupcakes with Almond Crunch (**PAGE 171**)

FENNEL & WHITE BEAN SOUP
WITH CRISPY PROSCIUTTO & GOLDEN CROUTONS

PREP TIME	START-TO-FINISH	MAKE AHEAD
25 minutes	1 hour, 10 minutes	Partially

THIS RUSTIC SOUP *with its rich, earthy flavors tastes as if you spent all day simmering it, but the truth is that it can be prepared in just a little more than an hour. Using canned beans that have been rinsed and drained saves a big chunk of time, and pairing them with fresh fennel in a simple broth enhances their flavor considerably. The saltiness of sautéed prosciutto and the crunch of homemade croutons as garnishes add another layer of flavor and texture to this dish.*

IN A LARGE, HEAVY SAUCEPAN over medium heat, heat the oil until hot. Add the fennel, onion, carrot, and garlic and sauté, stirring often, until just softened and translucent, 5 to 6 minutes. Stir in the crushed fennel seeds, a pinch of salt, and several grinds of pepper.

ADD THE BEANS AND BROTH. Bring the mixture to a simmer, then reduce the hea to low and simmer until the vegetables are tender, about 20 minutes.

REMOVE 1 CUP OF THE SOUP and purée it in a food processor or blender until smooth. Whisk the puréed mixture back into the soup to thicken it. Stir in the wine and rosemary and simmer the soup 5 minutes. Season the soup with salt and pepper to taste. (Soup can be prepared one day ahead. Cook to this stage; cool, cover, and refrigerate. Reheat over medium heat, stirring occasionally.)

FOR THE GARNISHES, to a medium, heavy skillet over medium heat, add 1 tablespoon of the oil. When hot, add the prosciutto and sauté, stirring with a fork (to help separate the strips if you stacked them before slicing) until crisp, 3 to 4 minutes. Remove with a slotted spoon and drain on paper towels. Add 3 more tablespoons oil to the same skillet and when hot, add the bread cubes. Stir until golden on all sides, 3 to 4 minutes. Remove and set aside. (Prosciutto and croutons can be prepared 1 hour ahead; leave uncovered at room temperature.)

LADLE THE SOUP into bowls and garnish each serving with prosciutto and croutons, and a sprinkle of fresh rosemary.

SOUP NIGHT MENU
Farmers Market Kale Salad with Pine Nuts and
Golden Raisins **(PAGE 115)**

Lemon Sorbet and Prosecco Parfaits **(PAGE 192)**

SOUP

2 TBSP olive oil

1 1/2 CUPS (1 large or 2 small bulbs) chopped fennel

1 CUP chopped onion

1 CUP finely diced carrot

1 1/2 TSP minced garlic

2 TSP fennel seeds, crushed *see page 203*

Kosher salt

Freshly ground black pepper

TWO 15.5-OZ CANS white beans, such as Great Northern or navy, drained and rinsed well

4 CUPS chicken broth or stock

3/4 CUP dry white wine

1 1/2 TSP fresh chopped rosemary

GARNISHES

4 TBSP olive oil

3 OZ prosciutto, thinly sliced and cut into strips 3 – 4 inches long

1 1/2 CUPS bread cubes (3/4 inch dice) made from a baguette or country loaf

2 TSP chopped fresh rosemary

TOMATO AND CHICKPEA SOUP
WITH YOGURT AND MINT

PREP TIME	**START-TO-FINISH**	**MAKE AHEAD**
25 minutes	*1 hour, 20 minutes*	*Yes*

IN LATE SUMMER, *when tomatoes are in their prime—deep red, juicy, and packed with flavor—consider making this simple soup. The tomatoes need only to be chopped and seeded, and then simmered slowly with chickpeas in a cumin-scented broth. Lemon, yogurt, and mint all contribute cooling accents to this soup, which is as good chilled as it is warm.*

IN A LARGE, HEAVY POT over medium heat, heat the oil until hot. Add the onions and cook, stirring often, until softened, 4 to 5 minutes. Add the garlic and stir 1 minute more. Add the tomatoes and chickpeas and sprinkle with cumin. Add the chicken broth or vegetable stock, tomato paste, 1 teaspoon salt, and cayenne. Bring the mixture to a simmer, and then reduce the heat to low. Simmer until the vegetables are tender, 35 to 40 minutes or more.

PURÉE THE SOUP in batches in a food processor, blender, or food mill, then return the soup to the pot. (Or use an immersion blender to purée the soup in the pot.) Stir in the lemon juice. If the soup is too thick, thin with 1/2 to 3/4 cup extra broth. Season to taste with salt and a pinch of cayenne.

IF SERVING CHILLED, cool, cover, and refrigerate at least 5 hours or overnight. Season it with more salt and cayenne if needed since chilled foods often require extra salt. (Soup can be prepared 1 day ahead to this stage: cool, cover, and refrigerate. If serving warm, reheat over medium heat, stirring often.)

LADLE soup into bowls. Garnish each serving with two tablespoons yogurt, swirling it over the top, and a sprinkle of mint.

SOUP NIGHT MENU

Vegetable Pitas with Whipped Feta and Orange Vinaigrette
(PAGE 144)

"Melt in Your Mouth" Lemon Rosemary Cookies **(PAGE 172)**
served with a bowl of fresh apricots

---

2 TBSP olive oil

3 CUPS thinly sliced onions

2 TSP chopped garlic

2 1/2 LBS ripe tomatoes, stemmed, halved, seeded, and cut into 1-inch dice

ONE 15.5-OZ CAN chickpeas, rinsed and drained

4 TSP ground cumin

4 CUPS chicken broth or stock *(or Quick-and-Easy Vegetable Stock, page 200), plus* more if needed

1 1/2 TBSP tomato paste

Kosher salt

1/8 TSP cayenne pepper, *plus* more if needed

3 TBSP lemon juice

1/2 CUP plain whole milk (not Greek) yogurt

4 TSP finely julienned or chopped mint leaves

FENNEL & CARROT BRODO OVER RED QUINOA

PREP TIME	START-TO-FINISH	MAKE AHEAD
15 minutes	*1 hour, 10 minutes*	*Yes*

QUINOA COMES IN VARYING HUES, *but I find the deep burgundy variety the most dramatic, and use it to anchor this flavorful brodo. I cook the quinoa separately, mound it in the center of bowls, and then surround it with a rich broth made with fennel and carrots. Both the quinoa and the broth can be cooked a day ahead so only a quick assembly is needed at the last minute.*

PLACE THE QUINOA IN A STRAINER, rinse under cold water, and drain well. In a medium, heavy saucepan (with a lid) over medium-high heat, add the quinoa and 1 1/2 cups of the chicken broth. Bring the mixture to a boil, then reduce heat to medium-low and cover. Cook until the quinoa is tender but slightly chewy, and white spiral-like threads appear on the grains, 12 to 15 minutes. Strain over a bowl, reserving any remaining liquid.

WHILE QUINOA IS COOKING, trim the stalks from fennel bulbs and reserve a few lacy sprigs in a glass of water for garnish. Quarter bulbs lengthwise and cut out tough cores. Cut each quarter crosswise into 1/4-inch thick slices to yield about 2 1/2 cups.

WHEN THE QUINOA IS COOKED, return it to the saucepan. Stir in butter, 1/2 teaspoon crushed fennel seeds, lemon zest, and Parmesan. Season quinoa with a pinch of salt if needed. Cover and set aside while you make the brodo. (The quinoa can be prepared one day ahead. Cook to this stage; cool, cover, and refrigerate. Reheat over low heat stirring constantly or place in a microwave proof bowl and heat in the microwave.)

IN A 4-QUART SAUCEPAN (with a lid) over medium heat, heat olive oil. When hot, add onion, sliced fennel, and carrots. Cook, stirring often, adding more oil if needed, for 4 minutes. Add garlic and remaining 1 teaspoon crushed fennel seeds, and stir 1 minute more. Add the remaining 5 1/2 cups broth plus any reserved liquid from the quinoa, and bring the mixture to a simmer. Reduce heat to low, cover, and cook until vegetables are tender, 12 to 15 minutes.

STIR LEMON JUICE into the broth and season with salt. (The broth can be prepared one day ahead. Cook to this stage; then cool, cover and refrigerate. Reheat over medium heat.)

TO SERVE, pack a 1/3 cup measuring cup or a small ramekin firmly with warm quinoa. Unmold it in the center of a shallow soup bowl. Carefully ladle broth and vegetables around (not over) the quinoa so that it holds its shape. Repeat to make 5 more servings. Garnish each serving with fennel sprigs and shaved Parmesan.

3/4 CUP red quinoa

7 CUPS chicken broth or stock

2 MEDIUM (about 10-oz each) fennel bulbs with lacy stalks

1 TBSP unsalted butter

1 1/2 TSP fennel seeds, toasted and crushed *see page 203*

1 TSP grated lemon zest

1/3 CUP grated Parmesan, preferably Parmigiano Reggiano, *plus* some shavings for garnish

Kosher salt

2 TBSP olive oil, *plus* more if needed

3/4 CUP chopped onion

3 – 4 MEDIUM carrots, halved lengthwise, and sliced into 1/4-inch thick half moons to yield 1 1/2 cups

1 TBSP minced garlic

2 TBSP lemon juice

SOUP NIGHT MENU

Romaine, Mint, and Creamy Ricotta Salad (**PAGE 119**)

"Melt in Your Mouth" Lemon Rosemary Cookies (**PAGE 172**)

NEW ORLEANS RED BEANS & RICE SOUP
WITH SCALLION-BACON GARNISH

PREP TIME	START-TO-FINISH	MAKE AHEAD
20 minutes	*1 hour*	*Yes*

RED BEANS AND RICE, *that beloved Louisiana mainstay, has been a favorite of mine for years since it was a staple of my Southern childhood. Typically this dish takes several hours to prepare since you must soak dried beans in water, and then simmer them with ham and seasonings for several hours. For this soup variation, I made some changes that reduced the cooking time. Well-rinsed canned beans, a real time saver, are cooked in a spicy stock for less than 30 minutes, and then ladled over bowls of rice. Crumbled bacon and chopped scallions make quick and simple garnishes.*

IN A HEAVY, LARGE POT over medium-low heat, fry the bacon until golden and crisp, 5 to 6 minutes. Remove with a slotted spoon and drain on paper towels. Chop coarsely and reserve for the garnish.

LEAVE 2 TEASPOONS of the drippings in the pot and discard the rest. Add the olive oil and set over medium heat. When hot, add the onions and sauté, stirring, until softened and lightly browned, about 5 minutes. Add the garlic and cook, stirring, 1 minute more. Stir in the tarragon, 1 teaspoon salt, cayenne, broth, beans, vinegar, mustard, and Tabasco sauce. Cook, uncovered, until soup has reduced by about one-third, about 15 minutes.

IN A SMALL BOWL, whisk the flour with 1 1/2 tablespoons water to form a loose paste. Whisk 2 tablespoons of the warm broth from the pot into the flour mixture, then whisk this mixture into the soup, stirring constantly, until it thickens slightly, 3 to 4 minutes. Season the soup with salt to taste. (The soup can be prepared one day ahead. Cook to this stage; cool, cover, and refrigerate. Reheat over medium heat, adding more broth to thin it if needed.)

TO SERVE, mound 3/4 cup rice in the center of shallow soup bowls. Ladle soup around the rice. Garnish each serving with a sprinkle of crumbled bacon, scallions, and parsley.

MARKET NOTE If you don't have tarragon vinegar, use white wine vinegar and add a generous extra pinch of dried tarragon to the beans.

SOUP NIGHT MENU

Oak Leaf and Apple Salad with Honey Cider Dressing
(PAGE 121)

Chocolate Cupcakes with Almond Crunch
(PAGE 171)

---

6 SLICES smoked bacon (6 – 7 oz) cut crosswise into 1-inch pieces

2 TBSP olive oil

1 1/2 CUPS chopped onion

1 TBSP minced garlic

1 TBSP dried tarragon

Kosher salt

1/8 TSP cayenne pepper *(or more for a spicier taste)*

4 CUPS beef broth or stock

TWO 15-OZ CANS dark red kidney beans, rinsed well and drained

1 TBSP tarragon vinegar *see Market Note*

2 TSP Dijon mustard

1/2 TSP Tabasco sauce

1 1/2 tbsp flour

3 CUPS cooked long-grain white rice *(Basmati rice works well)*

1/2 CUP chopped scallions, including 2 inches of green stems

4 TSP chopped flat leaf parsley

HARIRA
MOROCCAN LENTIL, CHICKPEA & LAMB SOUP

PREP TIME	START-TO-FINISH	MAKE AHEAD
20 minutes	1 hour, 15 minutes	Yes

FOR YEARS, *my husband and I ate only couscous and tagines when we frequented Moroccan restaurants during stays in Paris. Then one night we ventured farther afield, ordering harira, a classic soup prepared with lentils, chickpeas, and a touch of lamb. The soup was a revelation—light, yet totally satisfying, refreshing yet complex in flavor. There are many variations, but the constants include legumes and meat, a generous amount of cilantro and parsley, plus tomatoes and spices. In Morocco, the soup is often served at sundown to break the fast during Ramadan.*

IN A LARGE, HEAVY POT over medium heat, heat 2 tablespoons of the oil until very hot. Add the lamb and sauté, turning often, until nicely browned, 4 to 5 minutes. With a slotted spoon, transfer to a plate.

TO THE SAME POT, add remaining tablespoon of oil. When hot, add the onion and cook, stirring often, until translucent, 2 to 3 minutes. Add ginger and turmeric and stir 30 seconds. Return the lamb to the pot along with the cinnamon stick, 1 teaspoon salt, 4 cups water, tomatoes with their juices, and lentils. Bring to a simmer. Reduce heat to low, cover, and simmer 25 minutes. Remove and discard the cinnamon stick.

ADD 1/2 CUP CILANTRO, parsley, and chickpeas and cook 15 minutes. Stir in lemon juice. Season the soup with salt to taste. (Soup can be prepared one day ahead. Cook to this stage; cool, cover, and refrigerate. Reheat, stirring often, over medium heat. If the soup is too thick, thin with water.)

LADLE INTO BOWLS, garnish each serving with a sprinkle of cilantro, and a lemon wedge.

SOUP NIGHT MENU

Vegetable Pitas with Whipped Feta and
Orange Vinaigrette (**PAGE 144**)
or Smashed Chickpeas and Roasted Tomatoes
on Baguette Slices (**PAGE 149**)

Dark Chocolate Pistachio Brownies with
Chocolate Glaze (**PAGE 168**)

---

3 TBSP olive oil

6 – 7-OZ piece boneless leg of lamb, excess fat trimmed and discarded, cut into 1/2-inch dice to yield 3/4 cup

1/2 CUP chopped onion

1 TSP ground ginger

1/4 TSP turmeric

1 cinnamon stick, broken in half

Kosher salt

ONE 14.5-OZ CAN diced tomatoes with their juices

1/3 CUP (2 oz) green lentils

1/2 CUP chopped cilantro, *plus* **1 1/2 TSP** for garnish

1/4 CUP chopped flat leaf parsley

3/4 CUP cooked chickpeas, rinsed well and drained

1 TSP lemon juice, *plus* **4** lemon wedges, for garnish

SPICY RED LENTIL SOUP
WITH BUTTERNUT SQUASH & CAULIFLOWER

PREP TIME	START-TO-FINISH	MAKE AHEAD
25 minutes	_1 hour, 20 minutes_	_Partially_

I'VE OFTEN TOLD MY STUDENTS _that I could become a vegetarian if I lived in India. I love the way that country's cooks take humble ingredients like okra, potatoes, spinach, and lentils and transform them with fragrant spices, yogurt, and fresh herbs. The following recipe is a good example. Red lentils, or dhal, and a medley of winter vegetables are simmered with spices in stock until tender. As they cook, the lentils lose their coral hue, and break down into a rough purée that thickens this soup._

IN A LARGE, HEAVY POT (with a lid) over medium heat, heat 2 tablespoons of oil until hot. Add squash and cook, stirring often, until cubes are browned lightly and slightly tender, 5 to 6 minutes. Remove and set aside.

IN THE SAME POT, heat 2 more tablespoons of oil until hot. Add cauliflower, and cook, stirring often, until lightly browned and slightly tender, about 4 minutes. Remove and set aside.

IN THE SAME POT, heat the remaining oil until hot. Add onions and cook, stirring often, until slightly softened, 2 to 3 minutes. Add curry powder, ginger, cumin, and several grinds of black pepper, and stir 30 seconds. Add lentils, garlic, and 4 cups of the chicken broth or vegetable stock. Bring soup to a simmer. Reduce heat to low, cover, and simmer until lentils start to break down and lose their color and mixture thickens, 15 to 20 minutes.

STIR IN SQUASH, cauliflower, and remaining 1 cup of broth or stock. Cook, stirring occasionally, until the vegetables are very tender, 4 to 5 minutes. (Soup can be prepared two days ahead. Cook to this stage; cool, cover, and refrigerate. Reheat, stirring, over low heat.)

ADD SPINACH, stirring 1 to 2 minutes, until wilted. If soup is too thick, thin with a few tablespoons of broth. Season with salt and a pinch of curry if needed.

LADLE SOUP into bowls and garnish each serving with a dollop of yogurt and a generous sprinkle of cilantro.

6 TBSP canola oil

2 CUPS cubed (1/2-inch dice) butternut squash _or same quantity of pre-cut squash_

2 CUPS cauliflower florets, cut lengthwise into 1/2-inch slices _packaged florets work fine_

1 CUP chopped onion

1 1/2 TSP curry powder, _plus_ more if desired

1 1/4 TSP ground ginger

1 TSP ground cumin

Freshly ground black pepper

1 CUP red lentils

2 TSP minced garlic

5 CUPS chicken broth or stock _(or Quick-and-Easy Vegetable Stock, page 200), plus_ more if needed

2 CUPS (packed) baby spinach leaves

Kosher salt

1 CUP Greek-style yogurt

1/4 CUP chopped cilantro

SOUP NIGHT MENU

Shredded Romaine and Cucumbers with
Lime Dressing _(omit the peanuts and substitute diced mangoes for avocados for a more traditionally Indian preparation.)_
(PAGE 132)

Chocolate Cashew Brownies
with Chocolate Crème Fraîche Glaze
(PAGE 161)

COLORADO CHICKEN SOUP

<u>WITH</u> BLACK BEANS, CORN & PEPITAS

PREP TIME	START-TO-FINISH	MAKE AHEAD
25 minutes	*1 hour*	*Yes*

MY ASSISTANT, EMILY BELL, *created this soup while visiting her son and daughter-in-law and their two young children who live in the mountains of Colorado. Since both parents work on the ski slopes, this comforting soup was a big hit after long days outdoors. It is based around a flavorful tomato and chicken stock to which shredded chicken, black beans, and corn are added. A garnish of toasted pepitas and cilantro blended in a food processor (like a pesto but without any oil) tops each serving.*

IN A LARGE, HEAVY POT over medium-high heat, heat the oil until hot. Add onions, celery, carrots, and garlic and sauté until vegetables are slightly softened, about 4 minutes. Add the oregano, cumin, and smoked paprika and stir 1 minute. Add the chicken broth, tomatoes with their juices, and chilies and their liquid. Bring to a simmer, reduce heat to low, and simmer 15 minutes.

ADD THE CHICKEN, black beans, and corn and simmer 5 minutes more. Season the soup with salt and pepper. (The soup can be prepared two days ahead. Cook to this stage; then cool, cover, and refrigerate. Reheat, stirring often, over medium heat.)

PLACE PEPITAS AND CILANTRO in a food processor, and pulse until finely minced, scraping the bowl as needed.

LADLE SOUP INTO BOWLS and garnish each serving with a generous spoonful of the pepita mixture.

MARKET NOTE You can use a good quality rotisserie chicken from your local supermarket. A 2 to 2 1/2 pound chicken will yield 4 cups white and dark meat. Pull meat off bones and shred or cut into thin strips.

COOKING TIP If using frozen corn, defrost and pat it dry, then sauté the kernels in 2 tablespoons olive oil in a medium skillet over medium heat. Stir often until the corn is lightly browned, 4 to 5 minutes. This will bring out the sweetness of the corn.

2 TBSP olive oil

1 CUP chopped onion

2/3 CUP finely diced celery

1/2 CUP finely diced carrots

2 LARGE cloves garlic, minced

1 1/2 TSP dried oregano

1 TSP ground cumin

1 TSP Spanish smoked paprika *see page 203*

6 CUPS chicken broth or stock

ONE 28-OZ CAN diced tomatoes with their juices

ONE 4 – 4 1/2-OZ CAN chopped mild green chilies and any liquid

4 CUPS shredded cooked chicken *see Market Note*

ONE 15-OZ CAN black beans, rinsed and drained

2 CUPS fresh or frozen corn kernels *see Cooking Tip*

Kosher salt

Freshly ground black pepper

1/2 CUP roasted pepitas *see page 202*

1/3 CUP packed cilantro leaves

SOUP NIGHT MENU

Romaine, Avocado, Tomato, and Queso Fresco
in Cumin Lime Dressing (**PAGE 122**)

Three-Layer Chocolate Caramel Bars (**PAGE 159**)

"MIDNIGHT IN PARIS" ONION
SOUP GRATINÉ

CHIPOTLE BEEF AND BLACK
BEAN CHILI *topped with orange
sour cream*

CHICKEN NOODLE SOUP *with
sautéed mushrooms and parmigiano*

CREAMY CHICKEN SOUP *with
autumn vegetables*

RED CABBAGE AND
APPLE SOUP *with crispy bacon
and horseradish sour cream*

MUSHROOM SOUP "EN CROÛTE"

AFTER-THANKSGIVING TURKEY,
SWEET POTATO, AND BACON
CHOWDER

WINTER SOUP *from the chalet*

CAULIFLOWER SOUP *with crispy
chorizo, lime, and cilantro*

TOMATO, FENNEL, AND ITALIAN
SAUSAGE ZUPPA *with polenta
medallions*

4

·············

HEARTY COMFORT SOUPS

SOUPS WITH BIG, BOLD, COMFORTING FLAVORS—spicy chilis, onion soup gratiné, cream of chicken soup, or turkey chowder, to mention a few —are natural all-in-one dishes. I especially love to make these types of soups when the temperatures drop here in New England. On cold or brisk nights, I turn to steaming bowls of Red Cabbage and Apple Soup with Crispy Bacon and Horseradish Sour Cream, or piping hot creamy Cauliflower Soup with Crispy Chorizo, Lime, and Cilantro. Both are meals in themselves and take the chill out of our frosty evenings.

The inspiration for several of the "comfort food" soups in this chapter comes from my travels throughout Europe. "Midnight in Paris" Onion Soup Gratiné is my special version of the French classic. Winter Soup from the Chalet, a peasant vegetable and bean soup with smoked sausage, could easily be served *après-ski* in the Alps, while Tomato, Fennel, and Italian Sausage Zuppa with Polenta Medallions is reminiscent of rustic Italian cooking. Closer to home, some of my American favorites get updates too: traditional chicken noodle soup is elevated with sautéed mushrooms and a dusting of Parmesan. Chipotle Beef and Black Bean Chili Topped with Orange Sour Cream is prepared with chunks of beef stew meat that are simmered in a spicy broth in place of ground beef.

In keeping with the comfortable, rustic nature of the soups in this chapter, I would not hesitate to serve most of these soups straight from the pot. Just stack the bowls and garnishes alongside, and have a ladle ready for dipping. Even the Mushroom Soup "En Croûte" and the Onion Soup Gratiné, both of which are ladled into ramekins and finished in the oven, can be served from the kitchen. Leave them on their baking sheets and set them on the counter top.

When designing the menus for these soups, I've kept in mind their hearty nature. Many of the sides I recommend are salads tossed in refreshing citrus dressings or bracing vinaigrettes. One final note: despite how robust the soups in this chapter are, I still have people clamoring for second helpings. So don't worry—these recipes make generous amounts so you can dip more than once into the soup pot.

"MIDNIGHT IN PARIS"
ONION SOUP GRATINÉ

PREP TIME	START-TO-FINISH	MAKE AHEAD
35 minutes	*2 hours, 30 minutes*	*Partially*

THE ULTIMATE COLD WEATHER DISH—*soupe à l'oignon gratinée*—*was the pièce de résistance of a popular winter cooking class called "Midnight in Paris" that I taught several years ago. This recipe is based loosely on the first onion soup I ever made from* Julia Child's Mastering the Art of French Cooking, Volume I. *The main difference is that I suggest using a quick short-cut beef stock instead of Julia's homemade stock.*

This is a soup where the quality of ingredients used for the topping matters. An aged Gruyère and slices of a good crusty baguette will add immeasurably to the dish's success. One last tip direct from Julia: She suggests stirring some small strips of Gruyère into the soup before adding the toasted bread slices. Those little strips melt as the soup simmers in the oven, melding beautifully into the onion broth.

PREPARE THE QUICK-AND-EASY BEEF STOCK on page 198. When the stock is made and strained, return it to the pot. Set the pot over very low heat, then cover it, and keep the stock warm at a very low simmer while you prepare the soup.

IN A 5-QUART HEAVY POT (WITH A LID) over medium-low heat, heat the butter and oil. When hot, add the onions. Cover and cook, stirring frequently, 15 minutes.

REMOVE THE LID and raise the heat to medium. Stir in 1 teaspoon salt, the sugar, and the flour. Cook, stirring constantly, scraping the bottom of the pan so that the flour does not burn, until the onions are rich golden (like the color of light brown sugar), 35 to 40 minutes or more. (While you are cooking the onions, the flour will start to darken too and the onions will cook down considerably. That's okay.)

WHEN THE ONIONS ARE DONE, add the simmering stock and 1/2 cup of the wine. Season the soup with salt and pepper, and a pinch or two of extra sugar if desired. Simmer, partially covered with the lid set ajar, 40 minutes more. With a large spoon, skim off any foam that forms. Add the remaining 1/4 cup wine and season the soup again with salt and pepper. (Soup can be prepared three days ahead. Cook to this stage, then cool, cover, and refrigerate. Reheat over medium heat.)

WHILE THE SOUP IS SIMMERING, prepare the baguette slices and the cheese topping. Arrange a rack at center position of the oven and preheat to 350°F.

SOUP

2 QT Quick-and-Easy Beef Stock *see page 198*

4 TBSP unsalted butter

2 TBSP vegetable oil

3 LB yellow onions, sliced 1/4-inch thick, to yield 10 cups

Kosher salt

1/4 TSP sugar, *plus* more if needed

1/4 CUP all-purpose flour

3/4 CUP dry white wine

Freshly ground black pepper

CONTINUED ⇢

BRUSH THE BAGUETTE SLICES generously on both sides with olive oil and arrange on a rimmed baking sheet. Bake until slices are crisp, 4 to 5 minutes per side. Remove and cool. (Baguette slices can be prepared two days ahead; store in an airtight container at room temperature.) Retain oven temperature.

ARRANGE 6 OVENPROOF SOUP BOWLS or ramekins on a rimmed baking sheet and fill them 3/4 full with the hot soup. Divide the slivered cheese among the bowls. Float 2 to 3 baguette slices on top of each serving, and sprinkle generously with some grated cheese. Depending on the size of your bowls or ramekins, you may have some soup, cheese, or croutons left over.

BAKE THE SOUPS until the cheese has melted and is lightly browned, 15 minutes. Watch constantly. If desired, run under a hot broiler to brown more, 1 to 2 minutes.

TOASTED BAGUETTE SLICES AND CHEESE TOPPING

18 baguette slices, cut about 3/8-inch thick

3 – 4 TBSP olive oil, *plus* more if needed

12-OZ piece good quality aged Gruyère grated to yield 1 1/2 cups and the remainder cut into slivers 1/4-inch by 1-inch long to yield 1/2 cup

EQUIPMENT NEEDED

6 ovenproof bowls or ramekins
(1 – 1 1/2 cup capacity)

SOUP NIGHT MENU

Oak Leaf and Apple Salad with Honey Cider Dressing
(PAGE 121)

Extra Easy Brown Butter Almond Cake **(PAGE 178)** *served with scoops of vanilla bean ice cream or a tart fruit sorbet*

CHIPOTLE BEEF & BLACK BEAN CHILI
TOPPED WITH ORANGE SOUR CREAM

SERVES
6

PREP TIME	START-TO-FINISH	MAKE AHEAD
20 minutes	_3 hours_	_Yes_

ALTHOUGH _it has the salient features of quintessential American beef chili, this version calls for stew meat instead of the usual ground beef. Chipotle chili provides a smoky accent, while orange-scented sour cream, red onions, and cilantro are vibrant garnishes._

IN A MEDIUM BOWL stir together flour, 1 teaspoon cumin, 1 teaspoon salt, and 1/4 teaspoon black pepper. Pat beef cubes dry with paper towels, then dredge, a few at a time, in the flour mixture, shaking off excess.

IN A 4- TO 5-QUART DEEP-SIDED POT (with a lid) over medium-high heat, heat oil until very hot. Add enough beef to fit comfortably in a single layer without crowding, and brown well on all sides, 5 to 6 minutes. Remove to drain on paper towels. Repeat with remaining beef, adding more oil if needed.

ADD onions, carrots, and yellow pepper to pan. Stir, adding more oil if needed, until lightly browned, 3 to 4 minutes. Add garlic and stir a minute more. Return beef to the pot.

STIR IN remaining 3 teaspoons cumin, oregano, chipotle chili powder, 1/2 teaspoon salt, several grinds of black pepper, broth, tomatoes, and tomato paste.

BRING MIXTURE TO A SIMMER, reduce heat to low, and cover. Simmer until beef is very tender when pierced with a sharp knife and mixture has thickened, about 2 hours. Stir chili several times so that the meat does not stick to the bottom of the pan.

ADD BEANS and cook 10 minutes more. Season chili with salt. For a spicier taste, add a pinch or two more of chipotle pepper. (Chili can be prepared two days ahead; cook to this stage, then cool, cover, and refrigerate. Reheat, uncovered, over medium heat, stirring.)

FOR GARNISH PLACE SOUR CREAM in a bowl and whisk in orange zest and juice. To serve, ladle soup into bowls and garnish each serving with a dollop of sour cream and a sprinkle of cilantro and red onion.

GARNISHES 1 cup sour cream; 2 tsp grated orange zest; 1 tbsp fresh orange juice; 3 tbsp chopped cilantro; 1/2 cup chopped red onion

---

SOUP NIGHT MENU

Romaine, Avocado, Tomato, and Queso Fresco
in Cumin Lime Dressing (**PAGE 122**)

Lime and Ginger Cream Cheese Bars (**PAGE 157**)

1/3 CUP flour

4 TSP ground cumin

Kosher salt

Freshly ground
black pepper

2 LB beef chuck stew
meat, trimmed of
excess fat and cut into
3/4-inch cubes

4 TBSP canola oil, _plus_
more if needed

1 1/2 CUPS
chopped onion

3/4 CUP finely diced
carrots

1 yellow bell pepper,
seeds and membranes
removed, finely diced

1 TBSP chopped garlic

1 TBSP dried oregano

1 1/2 TSP chipotle
chili powder, _plus_ more
if needed

4 CUPS beef broth
or stock

ONE 28-OZ CAN diced
tomatoes, drained

1 TBSP tomato paste

TWO 15-OZ CANS
black beans, rinsed
and drained

SOUP · 75 · NIGHTS

CHICKEN NOODLE SOUP

WITH SAUTÉED MUSHROOMS & PARMIGIANO

PREP TIME	START-TO-FINISH	MAKE AHEAD
20 minutes	*2 hours*	*Partially*

This chicken noodle soup is a far cry from those of my childhood. Several things give this version its delicious flavor. First, chicken breasts are poached in a rich, aromatic stock to form the foundation. A mix of earthy sautéed mushrooms provides an umami touch. And, finally, some dry vermouth balances the soup's richness.

ADD ALL THE INGREDIENTS for the Extra-Rich Homemade Stock to a large saucepan over medium-high heat, and bring the mixture to a simmer. Reduce the heat to low, cover, and cook at a simmer until the chicken is very tender when pierced with a sharp knife, about 1 hour and 15 minutes.

REMOVE THE CHICKEN from the broth and set aside to cool. Strain the broth, pressing down on the vegetables to release as much juice as possible; discard the vegetables. You should get 8 cups; if not, add enough water to make that amount. When the chicken is cool enough to handle, remove the skin and bones and cut into 1/2- inch cubes. (Chicken and broth can be prepared one day ahead; cool, cover, and refrigerate.)

FOR THE SOUP, remove 1 cup of the broth and place it along with the vermouth in a small saucepan set over high heat. Cook until the mixture has reduced by half. Set aside.

HEAT THE BUTTER and oil in a large pot set over medium heat. When hot, add the mushrooms and cook, stirring, until lightly browned, 4 to 5 minutes. Add the garlic and rosemary and stir 1 minute more.

EXTRA-RICH HOMEMADE STOCK

1 1/2 LB chicken breasts, with skin and bones

2 RIBS celery, sliced into 1-inch pieces

2 MEDIUM carrots, sliced into 1-inch pieces

1 MEDIUM onion, quartered

2 bay leaves, broken in half

2 parsley sprigs

2 thyme sprigs, or **1/2 TSP** dried thyme

2 QT reduced-sodium chicken broth

SOUP

1/4 CUP dry vermouth

2 TBSP unsalted butter

2 TBSP canola oil

8-OZ fresh mushrooms, such as shiitakes, oyster, and baby bellas, sliced *see Market Note*

1 TBSP minced garlic

3/4 TSP dried crushed dried rosemary *see page 203*

2 TBSP flour

4-OZ short, wide egg noodles

1/3 CUP half-and-half

Kosher salt

Freshly ground pepper

6 fresh rosemary sprigs or **2 TBSP** chopped parsley for garnish *optional*

1/2 CUP finely grated Parmesan cheese, preferably Parmigiano Reggiano

CONTINUED →

ADD ALL THE INGREDIENTS for the Extra-Rich Homemade Stock to a large saucepan over medium-high heat, and bring the mixture to a simmer. Reduce the heat to low, cover, and cook at a simmer until the chicken is very tender when pierced with a sharp knife, about 1 hour and 15 minutes.

REMOVE THE CHICKEN from the broth and set aside to cool. Strain the broth, pressing down on the vegetables to release as much juice as possible; discard the vegetables. You should get 8 cups; if not, add enough water to make that amount. When the chicken is cool enough to handle, remove the skin and bones and cut into 1/2- inch cubes. (Chicken and broth can be prepared one day ahead; cool, cover, and refrigerate.)

MARKET NOTE Some grocery stores sell packages of mixed, sliced mushrooms including shiitakes, baby bellas, and oysters. This is a convenient way to buy them. If unavailable, use 4 to 6 ounces shiitakes (stems removed and mushrooms sliced) and 4 to 6 ounces baby bellas (trimmed and sliced through the stems).

COOKING TIP When this soup is made several hours or a day ahead, the noodles sometimes absorb more of the liquid and make the soup thicker. Thin it with some purchased chicken broth if you like.

SOUP NIGHT MENU

Red Leaf and Belgian Endive Salad with Shaved Comté
(PAGE 114)

Three-Layer Chocolate Caramel Bars
(PAGE 159)

CREAMY CHICKEN SOUP
WITH AUTUMN VEGETABLES

PREP TIME	START-TO-FINISH	MAKE AHEAD
25 minutes	*45 minutes*	*Yes*

This is a perfect dish to serve when the first cool days of fall arrive. Like most cream of chicken soups, this one is thickened with a little flour, but fresh autumn produce— including butternut squash, Brussels sprouts, and baby bella mushrooms—enhance this version of the comfort-food classic. Leftover rotisserie chicken or roast turkey both work well in this recipe.

IN A LARGE HEAVY POT over medium heat, warm 2 tablespoons of the butter and the canola oil. Add the butternut squash and Brussels sprouts and sauté, stirring frequently, 3 minutes. Add the mushrooms, stir, and cook the mixture 3 minutes more. Add the leeks, 1/2 teaspoon salt, and several grinds of black pepper. Continue to cook, stirring often, until vegetables are lightly browned and just-tender, 2 minutes or more. Remove the vegetables and set aside.

TO THE SAME POT add the remaining 2 1/2 tablespoons butter and when melted, stir in the flour. Cook, stirring constantly, about 2 minutes. Add the broth, half-and-half, 1 1/2 teaspoons rosemary, 1/2 teaspoon salt, and 1/8 teaspoon freshly ground black pepper, and whisk until the mixture comes to a simmer and thickens slightly, 4 minutes or more.

RETURN THE VEGETABLES to the pot and add the chicken. Cook until the chicken and vegetables are heated through, 3 to 4 minutes. Taste and season the soup with more salt and pepper if needed. (The soup can be prepared one day ahead. Cook to this stage, then cool, cover, and refrigerate. Reheat over medium heat, stirring often. If the soup is too thick, thin it with a few tablespoons of stock.)

LADLE THE SOUP INTO BOWLS. If you like, garnish each serving with a rosemary sprig.

SOUP NIGHT MENU
Grilled Cheese Tartines (PAGE 138)
Chocolate Cupcakes with Almond Crunch (PAGE 171)

---

4 1/2 TBSP unsalted butter

2 TBSP canola oil

1 1/2 CUPS diced butternut squash cut into 1/2-inch cubes *or purchase same quantity of pre-cut squash*

4 OZ small Brussels sprouts, ends cut off, cut lengthwise into 1/4-inch-thick slices

4 OZ small brown or baby bella mushrooms, cut into 1/4-inch-thick slices

1/2 CUP thinly sliced leeks

Kosher salt

Freshly ground black pepper

2 1/2 TBSP flour

3 CUPS chicken broth or stock, *plus* more if needed

1 1/2 CUPS half-and-half

1 1/2 TSP crushed dried rosemary *see page 203*

2 CUPS cooked, cubed chicken cut into 1/2-inch dice

Fresh rosemary sprigs, for garnish *optional*

RED CABBAGE & APPLE SOUP
WITH CRISPY BACON & HORSERADISH SOUR CREAM

PREP TIME
20 minutes

START-TO-FINISH
1 hour, 15 minutes

MAKE AHEAD
Yes

Red cabbage and apples seem to have a natural affinity when they are cooked together. Here they are combined along with bits of smoky bacon to form the foundation of this deep, crimson-hued soup. Crushed caraway and fennel seeds deepen the flavor while cider provides a sweet note.

IN A LARGE, HEAVY POT over medium heat, sauté the bacon until it is browned and crisp, 3 to 4 minutes. Remove to drain on paper towels. Leave 3 tablespoons of the drippings in the pan, and discard the rest. Coarsely chop the bacon and reserve for the garnish.

ADD THE CABBAGE and onions and sauté, stirring, until cabbage has wilted and onions have softened, about 5 minutes. Add the diced apples and continue to sauté, stirring frequently, until slightly softened, 4 to 5 minutes. Pour in the cider and red wine. Stir constantly to scrape up any browned bits on the bottom of the pot, about 1 minute.

ADD THE BROTH, caraway seeds, fennel seeds, 1 teaspoon salt, and 3/8 teaspoon pepper. Cover and simmer until the cabbage is very tender, about 25 to 30 minutes. In a small bowl, whisk the cornstarch with 2 tablespoons cold water until blended. Gradually whisk into the simmering soup and continue whisking until the broth has thickened just slightly, 4 to 5 minutes. Season the soup with salt and pepper. (Soup can be prepared two days ahead; cook to this stage, then cool, cover, and refrigerate. Store the bacon separately in a sealable plastic bag and refrigerate. Reheat the soup over medium heat, stirring occasionally.)

IN A SMALL BOWL, whisk together the sour cream, horseradish, and 1 tablespoon of the chopped chives or parsley.

LADLE THE SOUP into bowls. Garnish each serving with a dollop of the horseradish sour cream, a sprinkle of bacon, and chives or parsley.

6 SLICES thick smoked bacon (about 6-oz) cut crosswise into 1/2-inch pieces

1 (about 2 lb) red cabbage, quartered, cored, and quarters cut crosswise into 1/4-inch wide strips

1 1/3 CUPS sliced red onion (quarter a peeled onion lengthwise, then cut crosswise into 1/4-inch-thick slices)

2 MEDIUM Granny Smith apples, peeled, cored, and cut into 1/2-inch dice

3/4 CUP apple cider

6 TBSP dry red wine

8 CUPS beef broth or stock, *plus* more if needed

2 1/4 TSP caraway seeds, crushed *see page 203*

1 TSP fennel seeds, crushed *see page 203*

Kosher salt

Freshly ground pepper

1 TBSP cornstarch

1 CUP sour cream

2 TBSP drained horseradish

3 TBSP chopped chives or flat-leaf parsley

SOUP NIGHT MENU

Grilled Gouda and Kielbasa on Rye (**PAGE 139**)
or Winter Greens, Roasted Beets, and
Walnuts in Orange Dressing (**PAGE 131**)

Chocolate-and-Almond-Studded
Shortbread Bars (**PAGE 170**) *or* Molasses Spice
Cake Squares (**PAGE 167**)

MUSHROOM SOUP
"EN CROÛTE"

PREP TIME	START-TO-FINISH	MAKE AHEAD
30 minutes	*2 hours, 30 minutes (including 1 hour in refrigerator)*	*Partially*

THESE INDIVIDUALLY PORTIONED SOUPS *are truly magical. A light yet rich mushroom broth is ladled into ramekins and then topped with pastry rounds made from puff pastry sheets that are enriched with some grated white cheddar. You can prepare these soups several hours ahead so that, at serving time, you need only pop them in the oven and watch as the flaky pastry becomes golden brown and domes slightly above the bubbly soup beneath.*

PLACE THE PORCINI in a medium bowl and cover with 1 cup boiling water. Let stand until softened, about 20 minutes. Strain the mushrooms over a bowl in a fine mesh sieve lined with paper towels, pressing down on them to release as much liquid as possible. You should get 1/2 cup liquid. Chop the porcini into large pieces. Set the porcini and the strained liquid aside.

IN A HEAVY, MEDIUM POT over medium heat, melt the butter. When hot, add the crimini, shiitakes, shallots, and celery. Sauté, stirring until mushrooms and vegetables are softened, 5 to 6 minutes. Add the garlic, rosemary, and sherry, and stir until the liquid is absorbed, about 1 minute more. Stir in the reserved porcini and the strained liquid, plus the chicken broth. Bring the mixture to a simmer and cook 5 to 6 minutes, just for flavors to blend. Season with salt to taste.

FILL INDIVIDUAL, ONE-CUP RAMEKINS with soup to within 1/2-inch of the top. (Be sure to leave 1/2 inch so that the soup does not touch the pastry topping.) Set aside to cool while you prepare the pastry rounds.

PLACE A PUFF PASTRY SHEET on a floured work surface and sprinkle 1/2 cup of the cheese evenly over half of the sheet. Fold the other half of the sheet over the cheese and press down with your fingers. With a rolling pin, roll the pastry into an 11-inch square. Cut out four pastry rounds, each about 5 1/2 inches in diameter (or 1/2-inch wider all around than the tops of the ramekins). Repeat with remaining pastry sheet and cheese. Cover and refrigerate the rounds for 5 minutes. (You will have 2 pastry rounds left over; wrap tightly in plastic wrap, then in foil, and freeze for future use—see Cooking Tip.)

1 OZ dried porcini mushrooms

4 TBSP unsalted butter

8 OZ crimini mushrooms, trimmed and sliced through the stems 1/4-inch thick

4 OZ shiitakes, stems removed and julienned 1/4-inch wide

1/2 CUP chopped shallots

1/4 CUP very thinly sliced celery

1 1/2 TSP minced garlic

1/4 TSP crushed dried rosemary *see page 203*

2 TBSP medium-dry sherry (such as Amontillado)

2 CUPS chicken broth or stock *Swanson works well in this recipe*

Kosher salt

Flour for the work surface

CONTINUED →

IN A SMALL BOWL, whisk the egg with 1 teaspoon cold water, and brush one side of each pastry circle with some of this egg mixture. Carefully place a pastry round, glazed side down, over each ramekin. Firmly press the overlapping pastry against the outside of each ramekin. Be careful not to press down from the top to avoid cutting the dough on the edge of the ramekin. Press the tines of a fork around the pastry sides to make it adhere tightly to each ramekin. Do not make any slits on the top of the pastry.

Brush the tops and sides of the pastry with remaining egg glaze and place the ramekins on a rimmed baking sheet. Refrigerate, loosely covered with plastic wrap, for at least 1 hour or up to 4 hours. (Soup can be prepared 4 hours ahead. Cook to this stage then keep covered and refrigerated until ready to bake.)

Arrange a rack at center position of the oven and preheat to 400°F. Remove the plastic wrap and bake the ramekins until the pastry has domed and is a rich golden brown, 20 minutes or longer.

ONE 17.3-OZ PACKAGE frozen puff pastry with two pastry sheets, thawed overnight in the refrigerator

1 CUP grated sharp white cheddar cheese

1 large egg

COOKING TIP You can turn extra puff pastry rounds and scraps into a quick appetizer. Gather them into a mass and roll out to a 1/4-inch thickness. Cut the pastry into 1/2-inch wide strips, then cut strips into 1-inch pieces. Place the pieces on a baking sheet and bake in a 400°F oven until golden and puffed, 15 to 18 minutes. Remove and cool slightly.

> ### SOUP NIGHT MENU
>
> Frisée Salad with Walnuts, Pears, and Goat Cheese Dressing
> **(PAGE 118)**
>
> Extra Easy Brown Butter Almond Cake **(PAGE 178)** *served with vanilla bean or ginger ice cream and fresh orange segments*

AFTER THANKSGIVING TURKEY,
SWEET POTATO & BACON CHOWDER

PREP TIME
20 minutes

START-TO-FINISH
50 minutes

MAKE AHEAD
Yes

I AM RARELY AT A LOSS FOR WORDS *except in the dental chair. As it turns out, my hygienist loves food, and often asks about recipes during cleanings. A few years back, during a visit before Thanksgiving, she quizzed me about turkey leftovers, suggesting that I create a chowder with them. As she scraped and brushed, I came up with an "After Thanksgiving" chowder with turkey and sweet potatoes, and when I was finally able to speak again, I proposed this dish. In this version sweet potatoes replace traditional white potatoes and turkey substitutes for shellfish. She couldn't wait to try it!*

IN A LARGE, HEAVY POT over medium heat, sauté bacon until browned and crisp, 3 to 4 minutes. Remove to drain on paper towels. Crumble it coarsely and set aside. Leave 2 tablespoons of drippings in the pan and discard the rest.

ADD onion and celery to the pot, and sauté, stirring, 2 minutes. Then add sweet potatoes, 3/4 teaspoon salt, and 1/2 teaspoon pepper. Cook, stirring, until slightly softened, 3 to 4 minutes. Sprinkle flour over vegetables and stir constantly to cook the flour for 1 1/2 minutes.

ADD broth, sage, and thyme, and bring mixture to a simmer. Reduce the heat and simmer until vegetables are tender but not mushy, about 10 minutes.

WHISK IN HALF-AND-HALF, bring the soup to a simmer, and cook 1 minute. Add turkey and cook to heat through, about 2 minutes. Taste and season chowder with more salt and pepper if needed. (The chowder can be prepared one day ahead. Cook to this stage, then cool, cover, and refrigerate. Reheat over medium heat, stirring often.)

LADLE CHOWDER INTO BOWLS. Garnish each serving with crumbled bacon and, if desired, a fresh sage and thyme sprig.

MARKET NOTE Two types of sweet potatoes are available in the United States. One has pale tan skin and light colored orange flesh, while the other (often erroneously labeled as a yam) has a darker skin and rich copper-hued flesh. The latter variety is the one I like to use in this chowder. About 3/4 pound should yield 2 diced cups.

5 SLICES smoked bacon

1 CUP chopped onion

3/4 CUP chopped celery

2 CUPS (about 3/4 lb) cubed sweet potato cut into 1/2-inch dice *see Market Note*

Kosher salt

Freshly ground black pepper

3 TBSP flour

4 CUPS chicken or turkey broth or stock

1/2 TSP dried rubbed sage

1/4 TSP dried thyme

1 1/2 CUPS half-and-half

2 – 2 1/2 CUPS roasted turkey, cut into 1/2-inch dice

Fresh sage and thyme sprigs, for garnish *optional*

SOUP NIGHT MENU

Frisée Salad with Walnuts, Pears, and Goat Cheese Dressing
(PAGE 118)

Pumpkin "Brownies" with Maple Cream Cheese
Frosting **(PAGE 164)** *or* Chocolate-and-Almond-Studded
Shortbread Bars **(PAGE 170)**

WINTER SOUP
FROM THE CHALET

PREP TIME	**START-TO-FINISH**	**MAKE AHEAD**
35 minutes	*1 hour, 25 minutes*	*Yes*

This glorious winter soup is prepared with a mix of cold-weather vegetables that are paired with cannellini beans and bits of smoked sausage. The recipe is based on a soupe du chalet *that I spotted several years ago in a French cookbook. Although I am not a skier and have never spent a night in a chalet, I love the idea of robust après ski dishes like this one, and couldn't wait to try it. Rustic, warm, and satisfying, this potage exceeded my expectations. It improves in flavor when made a day ahead and needs only to be reheated at serving time.*

TO A HEAVY, MEDIUM POT (WITH A LID) over medium heat, add the olive oil. When hot, add the diced sausage and cook, stirring often until lightly browned, 5 to 6 minutes. Remove with a slotted spoon and drain on paper towels.

LEAVE 2 TABLESPOONS of the drippings in the pan and discard the rest. Return the pot to medium heat. Add the onion and leeks, stirring often for 2 minutes. Add the turnip and carrots; stir and cook until just slightly tender, 4 minutes or more. Add the broth and bring mixture to a simmer. Reduce heat to low and cook, covered, at a simmer until vegetables are tender, about 20 minutes. Add the potatoes and cook, uncovered, until tender, about 8 minutes or more.

STIR in the sausage and beans. Season with salt and cayenne. If soup is too thick, add up to 1 cup more broth. (Soup can be prepared one day ahead; cook to this stage, then cool, cover, and refrigerate. Reheat over medium heat, stirring occasionally. Thin with additional broth if soup has thickened too much.)

LADLE soup into bowls. Garnish each serving with a sprinkle of Gruyère and parsley.

MARKET NOTE Be certain you use a good quality smoked, cooked sausage. In the original recipe, a French pork sausage called Morteau was suggested.

> ### SOUP NIGHT MENU
> Winter Greens, Roasted Beets, and Walnuts in
> Orange Dressing **(PAGE 131)**
>
> Chocolate and Chestnut Pots de Crème
> **(PAGE 190)**

2 TBSP olive oil

8 OZ smoked kielbasa, cut into 1/2-inch dice *see Market Note*

1 1/2 CUPS chopped onion

1 1/2 CUPS (1 – 2 medium) chopped leeks, white and light green parts only

1/2 LB (about 1 medium) white and purple-tinged turnip, peeled and cut into 1/2-inch dice

1/2 LB carrots, peeled and cut into 1/2-inch dice

5 CUPS chicken broth or stock, *plus* **1 TO 2** cups more if needed

3/4 LB Yukon Gold potatoes, peeled and cut into 1/2-inch dice

ONE 15.5-OZ CAN cannellini beans, drained and rinsed

Kosher salt

2 PINCHES cayenne pepper

1 CUP grated Gruyère cheese

2 TBSP chopped flat leaf parsley

CAULIFLOWER SOUP
WITH CRISPY CHORIZO, LIME & CILANTRO

PREP TIME	START-TO-FINISH	MAKE AHEAD
20 minutes	1 hour	Yes

Although my mother served countless vegetables when I was growing up, she never cooked cauliflower. I, on the other hand, continue to marvel at the inventive ways a cook can use this vegetable. I've tossed the florets into pastas, incorporated them into creamy gratins, and used them imaginatively in soups like this one. For this spicy version, florets are simmered and then turned into a smooth puree. Lime-scented sour cream adds a cooling note and some pan-fried chorizo a bit of heat.

IN A HEAVY POT over medium-high heat, heat the olive oil until hot. Add the chorizo and cook, stirring, until slightly crisp, 4 to 5 minutes. Remove with a slotted spoon and drain on paper towels. Set aside. Reduce the heat to medium and add the leeks to the drippings in the pan. Cook, stirring often until softened, about 2 minutes. Add the garlic and cook, stirring, 1 minute more. Add the cauliflower, broth, and 1 teaspoon salt.

BRING THE MIXTURE to a simmer and cook until the cauliflower is very tender, 20 to 25 minutes. Purée the soup in batches in a food processor, blender, or food mill. (Or use an immersion blender to purée the soup in the pot.)

WHISK together the sour cream and the lime zest and stir half the mixture into the soup. Season the soup with more salt if needed and with 1/4 teaspoon or more black pepper. (Soup can be prepared two days ahead. Cook to this stage, then cool, cover, and refrigerate the sautéed chorizo and the sour cream separately. Reheat the soup over medium heat, stirring often.)

LADLE the soup into bowls. Garnish each serving with a dollop of the remaining sour cream. Serve with small bowls of chorizo, toasted breadcrumbs, and cilantro for sprinkling.

1 TBSP olive oil

6-OZ chorizo, cut into 1/4-inch dice *use Spanish-style chorizo in casing, not loose Mexican-style chorizo*

2 CUPS (2 – 3 medium) chopped leeks, white and light green parts only

2 TSP chopped garlic

8 CUPS (about 1 1/2 lb or use packaged florets) cauliflower florets

5 CUPS chicken broth or stock

Kosher salt

1/2 CUP sour cream

1/2 TSP grated lime zest

Freshly ground black pepper

Toasted breadcrumbs *see page 202*

1/4 CUP chopped cilantro

SOUP NIGHT MENU

Romaine, Avocado, Tomato and Queso Fresco in
Cumin Dressing **(PAGE 122)** *or* Chicken and Avocado Club
Sandwiches **(PAGE 146)**

Three-Layer Chocolate Caramel Bars **(PAGE 159)**

TOMATO, FENNEL & ITALIAN SAUSAGE ZUPPA
WITH POLENTA MEDALLIONS

PREP TIME	START-TO-FINISH	MAKE AHEAD
15 minutes	*1 hour, 20 minutes, plus 20 minutes for the polenta rounds*	*Partially*

THIS SOUP'S ROBUST FLAVOR PROFILE *comes from three complementary ingredients: sweet, fennel-scented Italian sausage, fresh fennel, and tomatoes. The sausage links are sliced so that they resemble petite meatballs, then browned and slowly cooked in broth along with tomatoes, fennel, and seasonings. It's the golden polenta rounds, though, that are set atop each bowl of the piping hot zuppa that complete this soup and turn it into a tempting all-in-one dish. This soup often cooks down faster than anticipated so feel free to thin it with additional broth if needed.*

WITH A SHARP KNIFE, cut the sausage through their casings into 1/2-inch pieces. In a large pot over medium heat , heat 2 tablespoons of the oil. When hot, add enough sausage to fit comfortably without crowding in a single layer. Cook, stirring and turning, until browned on all sides, 4 to 5 minutes. Drain on paper towels. Continue until all the sausage has been browned.

LEAVE 1 TABLESPOON of the drippings in the pot and discard the rest. Add the remaining 2 tablespoons of olive oil. When the oil is hot, add the leeks and fennel. Cook, stirring, until softened, 4 to 5 minutes. Add the garlic and stir 1 minute more.

STIR IN THE BASIL, crushed red pepper flakes, and 1/4 teaspoon salt. Add the broth, tomatoes and their juices, and tomato paste. Stir well and bring the mixture to a simmer. Return the sausage to the pan. Reduce the heat and cook until the sausage is cooked through and soup has reduced slightly, about 30 minutes. Season with more salt if needed, and thin with up to 1 1/2 cups extra broth if the soup is too thick. (Soup can be prepared two days ahead; cook to this stage, then cool, cover, and refrigerate. Reheat, stirring, over medium heat.)

TO SERVE, ladle the soup into bowls. Garnish each serving with 2 or more polenta rounds and, if desired, sprinkle with fresh basil. Pass a bowl of Parmesan cheese for sprinkling.

MARKET NOTE Look for sweet Italian sausage links that are seasoned with fennel seeds. When slicing the links, don't remove the casings; just use a sharp knife to cut them into 1/2-inch pieces. If using loose sausage, simply shape it into small balls about 1/2- to 3/4-inch in diameter.

1 LB sweet Italian sausage links seasoned with fennel
see Market Note

4 TBSP olive oil

2 CUPS (2 – 3 medium) chopped leeks, white and light green parts only

2 CUPS chopped fennel

2 TSP minced garlic

2 TSP dried basil

SCANT 1/2 TSP crushed red pepper flakes

Kosher salt

4 CUPS chicken broth or stock, *plus* up to
1 1/2 CUPS more if needed

ONE 28-OZ CAN diced tomatoes with their juices

3 TBSP tomato paste

Polenta Medallions
recipe follows

1/3 CUP julienned basil
optional

1 CUP grated Parmesan, preferably Parmigiano Reggiano

POLENTA MEDALLIONS

2 **CUPS** chicken broth
or stock

4 **TSP** unsalted butter

Kosher salt

Pinch of white pepper

2/3 **CUP** yellow cornmeal

Olive oil for brushing

ARRANGE A RACK at center position in the oven and preheat to 350°F. Have a greased rimmed baking sheet ready.

PLACE THE BROTH in a medium saucepan set over medium high heat. Add the butter, 1/4 teaspoon salt, and white pepper. Bring the mixture to a boil and slowly add the cornmeal in a very fine stream, stirring constantly with a whisk. After all the cornmeal has been added, simmer the mixture, stirring constantly until it pulls away from the sides of the pan, 5 to 7 minutes.

REMOVE THE PAN from the heat and immediately spread the cooked, thickened mixture onto a smooth clean work surface or a chopping board. Using a metal spatula, spread it into a circle about 1/2-inch thick. Let cool 15 minutes.

USING A 2-INCH COOKIE CUTTER, cut circles from the polenta. You should get 12 to 15. (You can gather remaining scraps into a ball and roll or pat them into another circle to make extra rounds if you like.) Transfer the rounds to the prepared baking sheet. (Polenta rounds can be prepared one day ahead; cover with plastic wrap and refrigerate.)

TO BAKE, brush the tops of the rounds lightly with olive oil. Bake until warm, 8 to 10 minutes. Watch carefully and do not overcook as the polenta can break down.

SOUP NIGHT MENU

Arugula and Shaved Fennel Salad in Lemon Dressing
(PAGE 135)

Lemon Sorbet and Prosecco Parfaits **(PAGE 192)**
or Florentine Sundaes **(PAGE 191)**

WARM OR COOL CARROT SOUP
with coconut and lime

COCONUT SOUP *with chicken,*
lemongrass, and spring vegetables

WARM OR CHILLED CURRIED
CAULIFLOWER SOUP

EXTRA SMOOTH AVOCADO SOUP
with corn relish

YELLOW SQUASH SOUP
with mascarpone

"BLT" FRESH TOMATO SOUP

END OF SUMMER VEGETABLE
SOUP *with parmesan basil toasts*

ICY-COLD WATERMELON SOUP
with whipped feta and mint

CUCUMBER "VICHYSSOISE"

MELON AND CUCUMBER
GAZPACHO

TOMATO GAZPACHO *with*
cucumber granita

LIGHT SOUPS—
WARM OR CHILLED

IN SPRING, when the weather turns warm and daylight reaches into the night, I change my soup-making ways. Instead of the hearty beans, lentils, winter greens, and smoked sausages I craved during the cold winter, I long for lighter fare. Mint and chives from my garden find their way to my kitchen and into my soup pot, as do the year's first asparagus and peas.

The fresh, aromatic soups in this chapter reflect this seasonal change. In the early days of spring when the weather can be mixed (warm one day and brisk the next), soups that can be served warm or chilled can bridge the gap between these seasonal extremes. Warm or Cool Carrot Soup with Coconut and Lime or Warm or Chilled Curried Cauliflower Soup or Yellow Squash Soup with Mascarpone each fall into this category. None demand seasonal produce (which might not yet be available) but all are, light and spring-like in taste.

When summer arrives, I can almost hear the vegetables growing in the fields in the nearby countryside: sweet watermelons, juicy crimson tomatoes, summer squash, fresh corn on tall stalks. The recipes in this chapter showcase the ever-changing, abundant produce available in the markets during this season. Cucumber "Vichyssoise" and End of Summer Vegetable Soup with Parmesan Basil Toasts, both prepared with summer's bounty, are two of my favorites.

On especially hot days, Avocado Soup with Corn Relish or Tomato Gazpacho with Cucumber Granita will rescue you from the heat. Neither requires any cooking. Just chop, assemble, and chill.

When making the chilled soups in this chapter, keep in mind that foods served cold often need extra seasonings to intensify their flavors. Taste as you go. And don't be afraid to reach for another pinch of salt or pepper or to add more herbs and spices.

WARM OR COOL CARROT SOUP
WITH COCONUT AND LIME

PREP TIME	START-TO-FINISH	MAKE AHEAD
15 minutes	*1 hour, 10 minutes, plus 5 hours if serving chilled*	*Yes*

DURING A STAY IN PARIS ONE SUMMER, *I noticed an unusual soup listed on the chalkboard outside a neighborhood café. I wasn't planning to eat lunch there, but was so intrigued by the sound of a carrot and coconut soup that I stopped in and ordered a bowl. Several minutes later, I was taking sips of a thick, creamy, orange-hued potage with wonderfully complex flavor. The chef had sautéed onions and carrots in butter, simmered them in chicken stock and coconut milk, then turned them into a smooth purée. Lime juice balances the carrots' sweetness and cilantro provides a nice herbal note. It couldn't be simpler to prepare and an unexpected bonus I discovered when I recreated this recipe myself is that it is equally good served chilled as it is warm.*

3 TBSP unsalted butter

1 1/2 CUPS chopped onion

1 LB carrots, peeled and sliced about 1/4-inch thick

ONE 13.5 – 14-OZ CAN light coconut milk *see Market Note*

1 1/2 CUPS chicken broth or stock *(or Quick-and-Easy Vegetable Stock, page 200)*

Kosher salt

4 TSP fresh lime juice

4 TSP chopped cilantro, for garnish

IN A LARGE, HEAVY SAUCEPAN (with a lid) over medium heat, melt the butter. Add the onions and sauté, stirring often, until softened, 4 minutes. Add the carrots and stir 4 more minutes.

ADD THE COCONUT MILK, chicken broth or vegetable stock, and 1/2 teaspoon salt and bring to a simmer. Reduce the heat, cover, and simmer until vegetables are very tender, 25 minutes. Purée the soup in batches in a food processor, blender, or food mill, and return the soup to the pot. (Or use an immersion blender to purée the soup in the pot.) Stir in the lime juice. Taste and season with more salt if needed.

IF SERVING CHILLED, cool, cover, and refrigerate at least 5 hours or overnight. After the soup is well chilled, taste and season with salt as needed since chilled soups often need extra seasoning. (The soup can be prepared two days ahead to this stage. Reheat over medium heat if serving warm.)

LADLE THE SOUP into bowls. Garnish each serving with a sprinkle of cilantro.

MARKET NOTE Light coconut milk is available in many supermarkets in the Asian section. Do not substitute cream of coconut, which is sweetened, for coconut milk, which is unsweetened.

SOUP NIGHT MENU

Crab Salad Sandwiches on Toasted White
(PAGE 152)

Crisp Oatmeal Thins Scented with Orange
(PAGE 162) *with ginger or vanilla ice cream*

COCONUT SOUP
WITH CHICKEN, LEMONGRASS & SPRING VEGETABLES

PREP TIME
35 minutes

START-TO-FINISH
50 minutes

MAKE AHEAD
Partially

WHEN MY ASSISTANT, DIANA TINDALL, *arrived at work one morning with this fragrant soup studded with bits of green, the aroma was so tempting that I quickly took a sip. Light in texture yet vibrant with Southeast Asian flavors, the soup was irresistible. Its base is prepared with chicken broth and coconut milk infused with salty, tart, and hot notes. Thinly sliced chicken, mushrooms, and snow peas are added to the simmering soup right before serving.*

IN A LARGE HEAVY SAUCEPAN, combine the broth, coconut milk, lemon grass, fish sauce, lime zest and juice, ginger, and red pepper flakes. Stir well and place over medium heat. When the mixture comes to a simmer, add the chicken and mushrooms. Simmer until the chicken is cooked through and the mushrooms are tender, 4 to 5 minutes. Season the soup with 1/2 teaspoon salt. (The soup can be prepared one day ahead. Cook to this stage, then cool, cover, and refrigerate. Reheat over medium heat.)

ADD THE GREEN ONIONS, snow peas, and peas and cook until the vegetables are just tender and bright green, 3 to 4 minutes. Taste and season with more salt if needed.

LADLE THE SOUP INTO BOWLS. Garnish each serving with the basil.

MARKET NOTE Coconut milk is available in many supermarkets in the Asian section. Do not substitute cream of coconut, which is sweetened, for coconut milk, which is unsweetened.

3 CUPS chicken broth or stock

TWO 13.5-OZ cans whole (not light) coconut milk *see Market Note*

1/3 CUP (3 – 4 stalks) finely chopped lemongrass *see page 203*

3 TBSP Thai fish sauce

1 TSP grated lime zest

2 1/2 TBSP lime juice

2 TBSP finely chopped fresh ginger

1/2 TSP red pepper flakes

1/2 TO 3/4 LB boneless, skinless chicken breast, sliced into 3-by-1/2 inch strips

6 OZ white mushrooms, cleaned and sliced very thinly through the stems

Kosher salt

1/2 CUP chopped green onions, including 2 inches of the green stems

4 OZ snow peas, trimmed and sliced on the diagonal into 2 – 3 pieces

4 OZ fresh or frozen peas

1/3 CUP julienned fresh basil

SOUP NIGHT MENU
Shredded Romaine and Cucumbers with Lime Dressing
(PAGE 132)

Extra Easy Brown Butter Almond Cake **(PAGE 178)**
with fresh diced mango and raspberries

WARM OR CHILLED
CURRIED CAULIFLOWER SOUP

PREP TIME
15 minutes

START-TO-FINISH
*1 hour, 10 minutes,
plus 5 hours if serving
chilled*

MAKE AHEAD
Partially

MARK TWAIN DESCRIBED CAULIFLOWER *as "cabbage with a college education." He had a point. This year-round vegetable has a more subtle taste than its humble counterpart. My guess is that Twain would have liked the way cauliflower is used in the following soup. Florets are simmered in a broth with assertive seasonings of pungent, sweet, and hot spices and then puréed. With its luscious smooth texture, this soup belies the fact that it is really quite low in calories. It is cooling and refreshing served chilled on a hot day, but just as tempting offered warm. Think of it as cauliflower with a Master's Degree.*

IN A LARGE HEAVY POT (with a lid) over medium heat, warm the oil. When hot, add the leeks and sauté, stirring, until just softened, 3 to 4 minutes. Stir in the cauliflower florets, chicken broth or vegetable stock, scant 1 teaspoon salt, curry powder, cumin, red pepper flakes, and cinnamon and bring to a simmer. Reduce the heat to low, cover, and simmer until the vegetables are tender, about 25 minutes.

PURÉE THE SOUP in batches in a food processor, blender, or food mill. (Or use an immersion blender to purée the soup in the pot.) Stir in the lemon juice. If the soup is too thick thin it with a few tablespoons of broth. Taste the soup and add more salt if needed.

IF SERVING CHILLED, cool, cover, and refrigerate at least 5 hours or overnight. After the soup is well chilled, taste and season with more salt if needed since chilled soups often need extra seasoning. (The soup can be prepared one day ahead to this stage. Reheat if serving warm.)

LADLE THE SOUP into bowls. Garnish each serving with a sprinkle of cilantro and toasted curried bread crumbs. Pass the extra bread crumbs in a small bowl.

2 TBSP olive oil

1 1/2 CUP
(2 – 3 medium) chopped leeks, white and light green parts only

1 HEAD (about 3 lbs) cauliflower, cut to yield 8 cups of florets or packaged cauliflower florets

6 CUPS chicken broth *(or Quick-and-Easy Vegetable Stock, page 200), plus* more if needed

Kosher salt

1 1/2 TSP curry powder

1/2 TSP ground cumin

SCANT 1/4 TSP red pepper flakes

1/8 TSP ground cinnamon

2 TSP lemon juice

4 TSP chopped cilantro

Toasted Curried Bread Crumbs *recipe follows*

TOASTED CURRIED BREAD CRUMBS

2 TBSP olive oil

1 TSP curry powder

1 CUP fresh bread crumbs *preferably made from a good artisan bread with crusts removed*

IN A SMALL BOWL, whisk together the olive oil and the curry then warm the oil in a medium heavy skillet over medium heat. When hot, add the bread crumbs and stir constantly until the crumbs are crisp and rich golden brown, about 3 minutes. (The bread crumbs can be prepared two days ahead. Store in a plastic, self-sealing bag at room temperature.)

SOUP NIGHT MENU

Chicken Salad with Fennel and Walnuts on Whole Wheat
(PAGE 153)

Chocolate-and-Almond-Studded Shortbread Bars
(PAGE 170) *with fresh apricots or plums*

EXTRA SMOOTH AVOCADO SOUP
WITH CORN RELISH

PREP TIME	START-TO-FINISH	MAKE AHEAD
20 minutes	*40 minutes*	*Partially*

ALTHOUGH AVOCADOS BOAST *distinctive characteristics like a smooth, beautiful texture and a gorgeous green color, their taste is fairly neutral. They work best paired with strong, bold flavors, as they are in this chilled soup. The fresh corn relish provides this counterpoint with its assertive flavors of lime, cumin, and cilantro. Place a dollop in the center of each serving, and pass the rest in a small bowl.*

FOR THE RELISH, in a medium skillet over medium heat, heat the oil until hot. Add the corn and onion and cook, stirring often, 4 minutes. Stir in the cumin and 1/4 teaspoon salt and cook until the onions have softened slightly and the corn is still crisp, 1 minute more. Stir in the lime juice. Transfer to a nonreactive bowl and cool to room temperature. (Relish can be prepared one day ahead to this stage; cover and refrigerate. Bring to room temperature before using.) Stir in 2 teaspoons of the cilantro. Taste and add more salt if needed.

FOR THE SOUP, place the avocados and buttermilk in a food processor or blender and process until smooth. Transfer to a large, nonreactive bowl. Stir in the ice water, lime zest, 1 1/2 teaspoons salt, and cumin. Taste and season with salt as needed since chilled soups often need extra seasoning. The soup is best made and served immediately so that the bright green color does not start to turn gray.

LADLE THE SOUP into bowls. Garnish each serving with some corn relish and a sprinkle of cilantro. Pass extra relish in a small bowl.

CORN RELISH

2 TBSP olive oil

2 CUPS (from 3 – 4 ears) fresh corn kernels

2/3 CUP chopped red onion

1/2 TSP ground cumin

Kosher salt

2 1/2 TSP lime juice

2 TSP chopped cilantro, *plus* more for garnish

SOUP

3 ripe avocados, halved, pitted, peeled, and cut into 1/2-inch dice

2 1/4 CUPS cold buttermilk

1 1/2 CUPS ice water

1 1/2 TSP grated lime zest

Kosher salt

3/4 TSP ground cumin

SOUP NIGHT MENU
Lobster BLTs (**PAGE 150**)
Cherries Poached in Red Wine and Spices
(**PAGE 182**)

YELLOW SQUASH SOUP
WITH MASCARPONE

PREP TIME	START-TO-FINISH	MAKE AHEAD
25 minutes	*1 hour, 10 minutes, plus 5 hours if serving chilled*	*Yes*

THIS SOUP IS TRULY EFFORTLESS *to prepare and can be served either chilled or warm. Sautéed squash and onions are simmered in stock and then puréed. The secret ingredient in this recipe, though, is creamy mascarpone that is swirled in as a final step. No one ever guesses that this is what gives the soup its velvety texture.*

IN A LARGE, HEAVY POT (with a lid) over medium heat, heat the oil until hot. Add the onions and sauté, stirring, until translucent and just softened, 3 to 4 minutes. Add the squash and cook, stirring constantly, 3 minutes. Add the garlic and dried basil and stir 1 minute more. Add the chicken broth or vegetable stock, 1 teaspoon salt, and red pepper flakes. Reduce the heat to low, cover, and simmer until the vegetables are very tender, about 12 minutes.

PURÉE THE SOUP in batches in a food processor, blender, or food mill, then return the soup to the pot. (Or, use an immersion blender to purée the soup in the pot.) Whisk the mascarpone into the soup a little at a time until well blended. Return the pot to medium heat and stir a few minutes to heat through. Taste and season with more salt and red pepper flakes if needed.

IF SERVING CHILLED, cool, cover, and refrigerate at least 5 hours or overnight. After the soup is well chilled, taste and season with more salt if needed since chilled soups often need extra seasoning to intensify their flavor. (The soup can be prepared one day ahead to this stage. Reheat if serving warm.)

LADLE THE SOUP into bowls. Garnish each serving with julienned basil. Pass a bowl of croutons for sprinkling over the soup.

SERVES 4

3 TBSP olive oil

1 1/2 CUPS chopped onion

1 1/2 LBS yellow squash, ends trimmed, halved lengthwise, and cut into 1/2-inch slices

2 1/2 TSP minced garlic

2 TSP dried basil

4 CUPS chicken broth or stock *(or Quick-and-Easy Vegetable Stock, page 200)*

Kosher salt

1/4 TSP red pepper flakes, *plus* more if needed

3/4 CUP (6-oz) mascarpone

4 TBSP finely julienned basil

Toasted croutons *see page 201*

> ### SOUP NIGHT MENU
> Summer Heirloom Tomatoes in Crushed Fennel Seed Dressing
> **(PAGE 125)**
>
> Buttermilk Panna Cottas with Blueberries
> **(PAGE 186)**

"BLT" FRESH TOMATO SOUP

PREP TIME
20 minutes

START-TO-FINISH
*1 hour, 15 minutes, plus
5 hours if serving chilled*

MAKE AHEAD
Yes

AFTER MAKING COUNTLESS BLT SANDWICHES, *I decided to interpret this trio of ingredients in a summery soup. The base is prepared with a fresh tomato broth brightened by the addition of orange juice, while garnishes of crisp crumbled bacon and ribbons of romaine complete the theme. Whether you serve the soup chilled or warm, use local tomatoes purchased from a farmers market or roadside stand for the best flavor.*

IN A LARGE, DEEP-SIDED POT over medium heat, fry the bacon until golden and crisp, 5 to 6 minutes. Remove with a slotted spoon to drain on paper towels. When cool, crumble or chop coarsely.

LEAVE 1 TABLESPOON of the drippings in the pot and discard the rest. Add the onion and garlic and cook, stirring often, until the onions are translucent and starting to turn golden, 3 to 4 minutes. Stir in the basil, 1/2 teaspoon salt, and cayenne. Stir in the tomatoes, broth, orange juice, and tomato paste and bring to a simmer.

COOK THE SOUP until the vegetables are tender, 15 to 20 minutes. Purée the soup in batches in a food processor, blender, or food mill, then return the soup to the pot. (Or use an immersion blender to purée the soup in the pot.) Season the soup with more salt and cayenne if needed.

IF SERVING CHILLED, cool, cover, and refrigerate at least 5 hours or overnight. After the soup is well chilled, taste and season with more salt if needed since chilled soups often need extra seasoning. (The soup can be prepared two days ahead to this stage. Reheat if serving warm.)

LADLE SOUP into shallow bowls and garnish the center of each serving with a generous dollop of sour cream and a sprinkle of orange peel, bacon, and romaine.

5 bacon slices (about 6 oz)

1 CUP chopped onion

1 TBSP chopped garlic

1 1/2 TSP dried basil

Kosher salt

1/8 TSP cayenne pepper

2 LBS ripe summer tomatoes, unpeeled, stemmed, seeded, and coarsely chopped to yield 4 cups

4 CUPS chicken broth or stock

1/4 CUP orange juice, preferably freshly squeezed

2 TBSP tomato paste

1/3 CUP sour cream

1 TBSP julienned orange peel *see page 203*

5 – 6 romaine leaves with ribs removed, cut into fine julienne strips to yield 3/4 cup

---

SOUP NIGHT MENU

Crab Salad Sandwiches on Toasted White
(PAGE 152)

Lime and Ginger Cream Cheese Bars
(PAGE 157)

END OF SUMMER VEGETABLE SOUP
WITH PARMESAN BASIL TOASTS

PREP TIME	START-TO-FINISH	MAKE AHEAD
30 minutes	_1 hour, 30 minutes_	_Partially_

WHEN AUGUST ROLLS AROUND _and friends with gardens begin dropping off zucchini in bushel baskets, use them in this vegetable soup. Along with diced tomatoes and orange bell peppers, they make a vivid mosaic in a light broth. A simple herbes de Provence blend of dried basil, rosemary, thyme, and oregano supplies the seasonings for this refreshing summer soup._

TO A LARGE, HEAVY POT (with a lid) over medium-low heat, add the oil. When hot, add the onion and sauté until softened but not browned, 4 to 5 minutes. Add the peppers and sauté 2 minutes more. Cover the pot and let the vegetables sweat for 2 minutes. Stir in the zucchini, cover the pot again, and sweat the vegetables for 4 minutes more. Stir in the garlic, basil, rosemary, thyme, oregano, 1/2 teaspoon salt, and 1/4 teaspoon black pepper. Add the wine and bring the mixture to a simmer. Cook, uncovered, until the wine has reduced by half, about 5 minutes.

ADD THE CHICKEN BROTH or vegetable stock, place the lid slightly ajar, and simmer the soup until the vegetables are very tender, 15 minutes.

REMOVE THE POT from the heat. Using a slotted spoon, transfer 3/4 cup of the vegetables to a food processor or blender. Add 1/2 cup of the liquids from the pot and purée. Then stir the purée into the soup to thicken it slightly.

RETURN THE POT to medium heat, add the tomatoes, and cook 1 minute so that the fruit do not lose its shape. Season the soup with salt to taste. (The soup can be prepared one day ahead. Cook to this stage; cool, cover, and refrigerate. Reheat over medium heat.)

LADLE THE SOUP into bowls. Serve with a plate of Parmesan Basil Toasts.

COOKING TIP Try to use small zucchini so that each piece will have some of the green skin. Trim and discard the ends of the zucchini, then quarter them lengthwise. Cut strips into 1/4 inch dice.

SOUP NIGHT MENU
Arugula and Sliced Fennel Salad in Lemon Dressing
(PAGE 135)

Individual Summer Peach Clafoutis
(PAGE 181)

---

1 1/2 TBSP olive oil

1 CUP chopped onion

3/4 CUP finely diced orange bell pepper

1 1/4 – 1 1/2 LBS small zucchini, cut into 1/4-in dice to yield 4 cups _see Cooking Tip_

1 TSP minced garlic

3/4 TSP dried basil

1/2 TSP crushed dried rosemary _see page 203_

1/2 TSP dried thyme

1/4 TSP oregano

Kosher salt

Freshly ground black pepper

1/2 CUP dry white wine

3 CUPS chicken broth or stock or Homemade Vegetable Stock _see page 199_

1 1/2 CUPS (1 LB) unpeeled, seeded fresh tomatoes, cut into 1/4-in dice

Parmesan Basil Toasts _recipe follows_

PARMESAN BASIL TOASTS
(MAKES 12 TOASTS)

2 TBSP chopped basil

3/4 TSP chopped garlic

6 TBSP olive oil

12 baguette slices,
cut 3/8-inch thick

1/4 CUP grated
Parmesan cheese, preferably
Parmigiano Reggiano

Fleur de sel

ARRANGE A RACK at center position and preheat the oven to 350°F.
Have ready a foil-lined baking sheet.

PLACE THE BASIL, garlic, and olive oil in a food processor or blender,
and pulse until garlic and basil are finely minced. Brush the baguette
slices on both sides with the basil/olive oil mixture and place them on
the baking sheet. Bake slices until golden and crisp, 3 to 4 minutes
per side. (Slices can be prepared 2 hours ahead. Keep uncovered at
room temperature.)

TOP EACH SLICE with some Parmesan cheese and return to the
oven until cheese has melted, 3 to 4 minutes. Sprinkle with a little
fleur de sel.

ICY-COLD WATERMELON SOUP
WITH WHIPPED FETA AND MINT

PREP TIME	START-TO-FINISH	MAKE AHEAD
15 minutes	*25 minutes, plus 2 hours or longer for chilling*	*Yes*

IN THE HEIGHT OF SUMMER *when watermelons are juicy and have a deep, rosy hue, consider enjoying them in an icy-cold soup instead of eating them by the slice. You don't have to turn on the oven or the stovetop; simply cube and purée the chunks with mint and lime. The salty whipped feta topping takes only minutes to assemble and contrasts well with the sweetness of the melon.*

PLACE THE WATERMELON in a colander and drain for 5 minutes. Transfer half of the watermelon to a food processor or blender, add 1 teaspoon of mint and pulse the mixture until slightly chunky. Transfer to a large nonreactive bowl. Repeat with the remaining watermelon and mint, and add to the bowl. Stir in the lime juice and zest. Cover the soup with plastic wrap and refrigerate until very cold, 2 hours or longer. (The soup can be prepared 6 hours ahead to this stage. Keep covered and refrigerated.)

FOR THE WHIPPED FETA, place the crumbled feta and cream cheese in a food processor and pulse until cheeses are blended. Pour in the olive oil and lime juice. Then process until the mixture is smooth, 30 seconds to 1 minute more. (If mixture is still lumpy, put it in a microwave-proof bowl and microwave it a few seconds. The heat will help the mixture become smooth.) Transfer the mixture to a bowl and stir in the lime zest. Taste and add more lime juice if needed. (Whipped feta can be prepared one day ahead; keep covered and refrigerated. Bring to room temperature 30 minutes before serving.)

TASTE the soup and season with more lime juice if needed since chilled soups often need extra seasoning. Ladle soup into bowls, and garnish each serving with a generous scoop of whipped feta and a sprinkle of julienned mint. Pass extra whipped feta in a small bowl.

SOUP NIGHT MENU
Chicken and Avocado Salad Club Sandwiches
(PAGE 146)

Chocolate Cupcakes with Almond Crunch
(PAGE 171)

SOUP

6 CUPS cubed, seedless watermelon (from a 5-lb or larger melon)

2 TSP chopped mint

2 TSP lime juice, *plus* more if needed

1/2 TSP grated lime zest, *plus* more if needed

WHIPPED FETA AND MINT GARNISH

6 OZ crumbled feta, at room temperature

2 OZ cream cheese, at room temperature, broken into small chunks

1/4 CUP olive oil

1 TSP lime juice, *plus* more if needed

1/2 TSP lime zest

2 TBSP finely julienned mint

CUCUMBER "VICHYSSOISE"

PREP TIME
20 minutes

START-TO-FINISH
*1 hour, 30 minutes, plus
5 hours for chilling*

MAKE AHEAD
Partially

THE EXPRESSION *"cool as a cucumber" comes from the belief that the interior of cucumbers stay several degrees cooler than the outside air surrounding them. They certainly have a cooling effect in this creamy soup, which is finished with swirls of yogurt and summer herbs. I like to use English cucumbers in this recipe because, along with having thinner skins and a milder taste, their seeds are much smaller and don't need to be scraped away. Served icy cold, this riff on traditional Vichyssoise might lower your internal temperature, too!*

CUT A 2-INCH PIECE from one of the cucumbers, and reserve it, unpeeled, for the garnish. Peel the remaining cucumbers, quarter them lengthwise, and cut into 1/2-inch chunks.

IN A LARGE, HEAVY POT over medium heat, melt the butter. When hot, add the shallots and sauté, stirring frequently, until they begin to turn translucent, 3 to 4 minutes. Add the diced cucumbers and stir to coat with butter. Cook 1 to 2 minutes. Add the broth and bring the mixture to a simmer. Reduce heat to low, cover, and simmer until the cucumbers are very tender, 20 minutes. Remove from the heat, uncover, and cool for 20 minutes.

PURÉE THE SOUP in batches in a food processor, blender, or food mill. (Or use an immersion blender to purée the soup in the pot.) Transfer to a bowl; add the yogurt, 4 teaspoons chopped tarragon, and 1 tablespoon chopped chives. Season with 1 1/2 teaspoons salt or more to taste. Process again in batches until mixture is smooth.

RETURN SOUP TO BOWL, cover with plastic wrap, and refrigerate until very cold, 5 hours or more. (Soup can be prepared one day ahead. Cover and refrigerate.)

TASTE AND SEASON with salt as needed since chilled soups often need extra seasoning. Add 1 1/2 teaspoons lemon juice. Then taste and add up to 1/2 teaspoon more juice if needed. Dice the reserved 2-inch cucumber piece into 1/4-inch cubes.

LADLE THE SOUP into bowls. Garnish each serving with diced cucumber, and sprinkle with tarragon and chives.

2 LARGE English cucumbers

4 TBSP unsalted butter

1/2 CUP minced shallots

2 CUPS chicken broth or stock *(or Quick-and-Easy Vegetable Stock, page 200), plus* more if needed

1 1/2 CUPS plain Greek yogurt

4 TSP chopped tarragon, *plus 2 TSP* for garnish

1 TBSP chopped chives, *plus 1 TSP* for garnish

Kosher salt

1 1/2 TO 3 TSP lemon juice

SOUP NIGHT MENU

Tuna, Hummus, and Kalamatas on Toasted Multigrain
(PAGE 142)

"Melt in Your Mouth" Lemon Rosemary Cookies
(PAGE 172)

MELON & CUCUMBER GAZPACHO

PREP TIME
20 minutes

START-TO-FINISH
*30 minutes, plus 3 hours
or longer for chilling*

MAKE AHEAD
Yes

A FEW YEARS AGO, *I sampled this chilled soup at the Cambridge Tea House in Columbus, Ohio, and was so taken with its refreshing taste that I begged the owner, Mary Boesch, to share the recipe. When the directions arrived, I was pleased to learn that this dish requires no actual cooking. The creation of Chef Sarah Jackson Wilson, it is prepared with diced cantaloupe and cucumbers that are puréed, then combined with lemon juice, cider vinegar, and Sriracha, the Thai counterpart to Tabasco sauce. That touch of heat enlivens the flavor, providing a nice balance to the sweetness of the melon.*

QUARTER THE CANTALOUPE, and scrape out and discard the seeds. Remove the skin and cut the melon into 1-inch chunks to yield 6 cups. (You may have some melon left over.) Peel the cucumber, halve it lengthwise, scrape out and discard the seeds, then dice into 1-inch chunks to yield 2 cups.

WHISK TOGETHER the vinegar, olive oil, lemon juice, and ice water in a medium bowl until blended.

PURÉE 1/3 OF THE CANTALOUPE, 1/3 of the cucumber, and 1/3 of the vinegar mixture in a food processor about 30 seconds or more and then transfer to a large nonreactive bowl. The mixture will be slightly chunky, not completely smooth. Repeat two more times with remaining cantaloupe, cucumbers, and vinegar mixture.

STIR IN 1 TEASPOON SALT and Sriracha. Cover and chill for at least 3 hours or overnight. After the soup is well chilled, taste and season with more salt and Sriracha as needed since chilled soups often need extra seasoning. (Soup can be prepared one day ahead. Keep covered and refrigerated.)

LADLE INTO BOWLS. Garnish each serving with a mint sprig.

MARKET NOTE Sriracha, a Thai sauce composed of chilies, vinegar, garlic, and salt, is available in many grocery stores and in Asian markets.

1 LARGE (about 4 lbs) ripe cantaloupe

1 LARGE (10 to 12-oz) English cucumber

1/4 CUP cider vinegar

1/4 CUP olive oil

2 TBSP lemon juice

3/4 CUP ice water

Kosher salt

1 TSP Sriracha, *plus* more if needed *see Market Note*

Fresh mint sprigs for garnish

SOUP NIGHT MENU

Toasted Baguette, Smoked Turkey,
Fontina, and Garlic Mayo **(PAGE 147)**
or Lobster BLTs **(PAGE 150)**

Blueberry Pan Cake with Lemon Crème Fraîche
(PAGE 176)

TOMATO GAZPACHO
WITH CUCUMBER GRANITA

PREP TIME	START-TO-FINISH	MAKE AHEAD
25 minutes	*1 hour, plus 2 hours or longer for chilling the gazpacho and the granita*	*Yes*

ON AN UNBELIEVABLY HOT *summer night in Paris when the temperature soared to 103°F, I made this gazpacho the centerpiece of a meal for friends. The recipe is a fairly classic preparation, but what sets it apart is its garnish—a cucumber granita. A mix of puréed cucumbers, Perrier, lime juice, and sherry vinegar, it is simple to prepare but adds an extra level of chill to the soup. This duo certainly cooled our group down on that steamy evening. We didn't leave the table for three hours, until a slight breeze finally wafted through the windows.*

FILL A LARGE SAUCEPAN two thirds full with water and bring to a boil. Using a sharp knife, make an "x" on the bottom of each tomato. Add them to the pan for 20 seconds. Remove the tomatoes with a slotted spoon and, with a sharp knife, peel and discard the skins. Stem the tomatoes, then quarter lengthwise and scrape out and discard the seeds. Transfer the tomatoes to a large bowl.

STEM THE BELL PEPPERS, then quarter them lengthwise and cut out and discard the seeds and membranes. Chop coarsely and add to the bowl with tomatoes.

ADD THE CUCUMBER, onion, garlic, and half of bread cubes to the bowl of vegetables.

IN A FOOD PROCESSOR OR BLENDER, process the vegetable mixture in batches until it is slightly chunky. Return it to the large bowl. Stir in 4 tablespoons olive oil, vinegar, lime juice, 2 teaspoons salt, and several grinds of pepper. Add the crushed ice. Cover and refrigerate the soup until icy cold, at least 1 hour or longer. (The gazpacho can be prepared one day ahead to this stage. Cover and refrigerate) Taste and add more salt if needed since chilled soups often need extra seasoning. If the gazpacho is too thick, thin it with 1/2 cup or more ice water.

IN A MEDIUM HEAVY SKILLET set over medium-high heat, heat 3 tablespoons olive oil until hot. Add the remaining bread cubes; stir and cook until the bread is crisp and golden, 3 to 4 minutes. Remove and set aside. (Croutons can be prepared 4 hours ahead; cover loosely with foil and leave at room temperature.)

LADLE THE GAZPACHO into bowls. Garnish each serving with a scoop of cucumber granita. Pass the croutons in a bowl for scattering over the soup.

CONTINUED →

2 LBS ripe summer tomatoes

1 MEDIUM red bell pepper

1 MEDIUM green bell pepper

1 MEDIUM cucumber, peeled but unseeded, and cut into 1/2-inch thick rounds

1 MEDIUM onion, cut into quarters

2 MEDIUM garlic cloves, coarsely chopped

3 CUPS bread cubes (1/2-inch dice), made from a good crusty country loaf such as *pain de campagne*

4 TBSP *plus* **3 TBSP** olive oil

1 1/2 TBSP sherry wine vinegar

2 TSP lime juice

Kosher or sea salt

Freshly ground black pepper

10 ice cubes, crushed

Cucumber Granita *recipe follows*

CUCUMBER GRANITA
(MAKES ABOUT 3/4 CUP)

1/2 cucumber, peeled, but unseeded, and diced to yield 3/4 cup

1/2 CUP Perrier, or other similar sparkling mineral water

3/4 TSP fresh lime juice, *plus* more if needed

1/4 TSP sherry wine vinegar

Kosher or sea salt

PURÉE THE CUCUMBER and Perrier water in a food processor or blender until smooth. Add lime juice, sherry vinegar, and 3/8 teaspoon salt, and process 5 seconds more. Transfer the mixture to an 8-by-8-inch Pyrex dish (or a shallow freezer-proof bowl). Cover with plastic wrap, and freeze for 1 hour. Then, with a fork, stir the mixture to break up any frozen chunks. Taste and season with 1/4 teaspoon lime juice and more salt if needed.

COVER AND FREEZE again until the mixture is firm, 2 to 3 hours. Every 30 minutes, stir and scrape the mixture with a fork to break it into icy flakes. Granità is best used the day it is made. (You can prepare it up to two days ahead. If it freezes solid, break into chunks and then pulse the chunks in a food processor for a few seconds until cut into shavings)

SOUP NIGHT MENU

Haricots Verts, Cherry Tomatoes, and Chorizo Salad in Sherry Vinaigrette **(PAGE 128)**

Rustic Apricot Tart **(PAGE 184)**

RED LEAF AND BELGIAN
ENDIVE SALAD *with shaved Comté*

FARMERS MARKET KALE SALAD
with pine nuts and golden raisins

RADICCHIO, SPINACH, AND
GRAPEFRUIT SALAD

FRISÉE SALAD *with walnuts, pears,
and goat cheese dressing*

ROMAINE, MINT, AND CREAMY
RICOTTA SALAD

OAK LEAF AND APPLE SALAD
with honey cider dressing

ROMAINE, AVOCADO, TOMATO,
AND QUESO FRESCO *in cumin lime
dressing*

SUMMER HEIRLOOM TOMATOES
in crushed fennel seed dressing

MARKET SALAD *with fresh peas,
radishes, and melon*

HARICOTS VERTS, CHERRY
TOMATOES, AND CHORIZO
SALAD *in sherry vinaigrette*

WINTER GREENS, ROASTED
BEETS, AND WALNUTS *in orange
dressing*

SHREDDED ROMAINE AND
CUCUMBERS *with lime dressing*

WATERCRESS SALAD *with orange-
ginger dressing*

ARUGULA AND SHAVED FENNEL
SALAD *in lemon dressing*

6

....

SALADS
FOR ALL SEASONS

WHEN I WAS GROWING UP, fresh salads did not make frequent appearances at our family table. I can still remember my mother's frozen fruit salad, a sweet mixture of canned fruits, marshmallows, nuts, and sour cream. She also served pickled beets and onions that were more a condiment than a salad. When we occasionally had a green salad, it was inevitably iceberg lettuce drizzled with a bottled dressing.

Maybe it is because of this childhood depravation, but ever since I began cooking several decades ago, I've valued the gift of a good salad. And what could accompany a bowl of soup—piping hot or icy cold—better than a fresh salad tossed in homemade dressing?

The salads in this chapter, which draw on a wide range of ingredients, have been created to pair with the soups on the preceding pages. They call for an extensive variety of greens—red leaf, oak leaf, romaine, kale, frisée, Belgian endive, watercress, to name a few—but none so exotic that they couldn't be found at a good grocery store or farmers market. The dressings are primarily vinaigrettes and citrus and oil pairings, but simple extras like crushed fennel seeds or a hint of maple syrup or honey intensify their flavor and make them more interesting.

For fall soup suppers, Red Leaf, and Belgian Endive Salad with Shaved Comté or Frisée Salad with Walnuts, Pears, and Goat Cheese Dressing are full of seasonal color. When the cold days of winter call out for robust menus, consider Radicchio, Spinach, and Grapefruit Salad or Winter Greens, Roasted Beets, and Walnuts in Orange Dressing. The Market Salad with Fresh Peas, Radishes, and Melon is a great dish to celebrate the arrival of spring, while the Haricots Verts, Cherry Tomato, and Chorizo Salad is a perfect summertime refresher with its bracing sherry vinaigrette.

Most of the dressings can be whisked together well in advance, and the lettuce greens cleaned and refrigerated several hours ahead. Other ingredients like toasted nuts and shaved or crumbled cheeses can be readied ahead, too. Tossing and dressing these salads is all that is necessary at serving time.

RED LEAF & BELGIAN ENDIVE SALAD
WITH SHAVED COMTÉ

PREP TIME	START-TO-FINISH	MAKE AHEAD
10 minutes	*25 minutes*	*Partially*

COMTÉ—*a firm, ivory-hued cow's milk cheese with a slightly sweet, nutty flavor from the Franche-Comté region in eastern France—makes a fine garnish to this winter salad. This cheese's sweet notes counter the tart Belgian endive while its smooth texture contrasts with the crunchy hazelnuts and crisp pears of the garnishes. Beautiful deep wine- and green-hued leaf lettuce adds visual punch to this salad tossed in a simple balsamic shallot vinaigrette.*

FOR THE VINAIGRETTE, in a medium nonreactive bowl whisk the vinegar, mustard, 1/2 teaspoon salt, and several grinds of pepper to combine well. Gradually whisk in the olive oil, then stir in the shallots. (Vinaigrette can be prepared one day ahead; cover and refrigerate. Bring to room temperature for 30 minutes, and whisk well before using.)

FOR THE SALAD, place the pear slices in a salad bowl and toss with half of the dressing. Marinate 5 minutes. Add the lettuce and Belgian endive and toss gently, with a little more dressing to coat the greens. (You may not need to use all of the dressing.) Season the salad with salt.

SPRINKLE with hazelnuts or walnuts. Then shave a generous amount of cheese over the salad. (You may have some cheese left over.)

BALSAMIC SHALLOT VINAIGRETTE

4 TSP balsamic vinegar

1/2 TSP Dijon mustard

Kosher salt

Freshly ground black pepper

1/4 CUP olive oil

1/4 CUP finely chopped shallots

SALAD

1 ripe (but firm) unpeeled pear, halved, cored, and thinly sliced

2 medium heads dark red leaf lettuce, baby romaine, or butter lettuce, torn into bite-size pieces

1 Belgian endive, halved lengthwise, and halves cut crosswise into 1/2-inch-thick slices

Kosher salt

1/2 CUP hazelnuts or walnuts, toasted and coarsely chopped *see page 202 or 203*

1 6-oz piece Comté cheese

FARMERS MARKET KALE SALAD
WITH PINE NUTS & GOLDEN RAISINS

PREP TIME	START-TO-FINISH	MAKE AHEAD
5 minutes	*15 minutes*	*Partially*

ONE DAY AT MY LOCAL FARMERS MARKET, *I was deciding whether to purchase a bunch of kale when the merchant interceded. Sensing my ambivalence, she encouraged me to try some by sharing her recipe for a kale salad with pine nuts and golden raisins. I was so tempted by the sound of this dish that I promptly tucked some kale into my basket. At home, I whisked together her lemon dressing seasoned with maple syrup and red pepper flakes, then tossed wide strips of the curly kale in it. Toasted pine nuts and golden raisins added crunch and sweetness respectively. From my first bite, I was crazy about this salad and have made it many times since. It pairs particularly well with fall squash or bean soups.*

FOR THE DRESSING, in a nonreactive bowl whisk together olive oil, lemon juice, syrup, mustard, 1/2 teaspoon salt, red pepper flakes, and 1/4 teaspoon black pepper. (The dressing can be prepared one day ahead; cover and refrigerate. Bring to room temperature for 30 minutes and whisk well before using.)

FOR THE SALAD, remove and discard the tough stems and center veins from the kale leaves. Then cut the leaves crosswise into 1/2-inch-wide strips to yield 8 cups.

TRANSFER THE DRESSING to a salad bowl and whisk well. Add the kale and toss to coat the greens thoroughly. Taste and season with more salt and red pepper flakes if needed.

MOUND salad on salad plates. Garnish each serving with raisins and pine nuts.

MARKET NOTE Kale comes in many colors and varieties. For this salad, I like the dark green variety with creamy white stems or the dark green with purple-tinged leaves and stems. Choose kale with firm leaves and store in the coldest area of your refrigerator for no more than two to three days before using.

LEMON MAPLE DRESSING

2 TBSP olive oil

1 TBSP lemon juice

2 TSP maple syrup

1 TSP Dijon mustard

Kosher salt

1/4 TSP red pepper flakes *more for a spicier taste*

Freshly ground black pepper

SALAD

8 OZ kale *see Market Note*

1/4 CUP golden raisins

1/4 CUP pine nuts, toasted *see page 203*

RADICCHIO, SPINACH & GRAPEFRUIT SALAD

PREP TIME	START-TO-FINISH	MAKE AHEAD
10 minutes	*40 minutes*	*Partially*

THIS COLORFUL SALAD *with its varying hues—deep crimson from radicchio, verdant touches from baby spinach, and rich purple from Kalamatas—has an unexpected but cooling accent of citrus provided by fresh grapefruit segments. It is a particularly good partner to rich, cold weather soups.*

FOR THE DRESSING, in a nonreactive salad bowl combine the vinegar, fennel seeds, 1/2 teaspoon salt, and several grinds of pepper. Whisk well to blend, then gradually whisk in the olive oil.

FOR THE SALAD, trim a slice from the top and the bottom of a grapefruit. Then, stand the grapefruit upright on a work surface and, with a sharp knife (starting at the top and bringing the knife all the way down to the bottom), cut off all the skin and the white pith beneath. Repeat with the remaining grapefruit. Slice segments from the grapefruits, cutting between the membranes.

ADD THE GRAPEFRUIT segments to the bowl with the dressing and toss to coat well; let stand at least 15 minutes or up to one hour so that juices from the grapefruit meld with the dressing. (The salad can be prepared to this stage one hour ahead; leave at room temperature.)

ADD the radicchio, spinach, and olives to the salad bowl and toss to mix. Taste and add more salt and pepper if needed. Mound the salad on a salad plate.

CRUSHED FENNEL SEED DRESSING

5 TBSP red wine vinegar

1 TSP fennel seeds, crushed *see page 203*

Kosher salt

Freshly ground black pepper

1/2 CUP olive oil

SALAD

2 red or white grapefruit

1 LARGE HEAD (about 10-oz) radicchio, torn into bite-size pieces

8 OZ baby spinach leaves

1/2 CUP Kalamata olives, pitted

OAK LEAF AND APPLE SALAD
WITH HONEY CIDER DRESSING

PREP TIME	START-TO-FINISH	MAKE AHEAD
20 minutes	*35 minutes*	*Partially*

FOR AN INTERESTING FALL OR WINTER SALAD, *try this combination of tender red oak leaf lettuce and tart frisée, paired with thinly sliced apple, fennel, and red onion. A simple dressing prepared with honey, cider vinegar, and mustard adds both sweet and tart notes. Because it has plenty of assertive flavors, I always pair this salad with big, bold soups such as the New Orleans Red Bean and Rice Soup or the "Midnight in Paris" Onion Soup Gratiné.*

FOR THE VINAIGRETTE, in a medium, nonreactive bowl whisk together honey, vinegar, mustard, and scant 1/2 teaspoon salt until blended. Whisk in oil. (Vinaigrette can be made one day ahead. Cover and refrigerate. Bring to room temperature for 30 minutes, and whisk well before using.)

FOR THE SALAD, add sliced apple, onion, and fennel to a salad bowl and toss with half of the dressing. Marinate 10 minutes. Add the oak leaf and frisée; toss with just enough of the remaining dressing to coat lightly. (You may have some dressing leftover.) Season salad with more salt and with a few grinds of black pepper to taste. Sprinkle walnuts over the top.

HONEY CIDER VINAIGRETTE

1/4 CUP honey

1/4 CUP cider vinegar

2 TSP Dijon mustard

Kosher salt

1/3 CUP canola oil

SALAD

1 firm, crisp, unpeeled apple *(such as Granny Smith)*, halved, cored, and thinly sliced

1/2 medium red onion, thinly sliced

1/2 medium fennel bulb, tough center core removed and discarded, thinly sliced

4 CUPS oak leaf or red leaf lettuce, torn into bite-size pieces

4 CUPS frisée or other tart greens *see Market Note, page 118*

Freshly ground black pepper

3 TBSP walnuts, toasted and coarsely chopped *see page 203*

ROMAINE, AVOCADO, TOMATO & QUESO FRESCO
_IN_ CUMIN LIME DRESSING

PREP TIME	START-TO-FINISH	MAKE AHEAD
20 minutes	_35 minutes_	_Partially_

WHAT I LOVE ABOUT THIS SALAD _is its versatility. I serve it with spicy chilis, with black bean soups, with corn chowders, and the list goes on. It's an old fashioned layered salad with updated ingredients. A layer of torn romaine leaves comes first, followed by a mix of avocados, grape tomatoes, and red onions. Finally, some snowy white queso fresco is crumbled and sprinkled on top._

FOR THE DRESSING, in a small nonreactive bowl, whisk together the lime zest and juice, garlic, cumin, 3/4 teaspoon salt, and several grinds of black pepper. Whisk in the olive oil. Taste and season with more salt if needed. (Dressing can be prepared one day ahead. Cover and refrigerate. Bring to room temperature for 30 minutes and whisk well before using.)

FOR THE SALAD, in a medium bowl toss the avocados, tomatoes, and red onion. Pour half of the dressing over them and toss again gently. Reserve remaining dressing for tossing with the lettuce. Marinate the avocado mixture for at least 10 minutes or up to 30 minutes.

IN A SHALLOW SALAD BOWL or in a large shallow serving dish, toss the romaine with just enough of the remaining dressing to coat it lightly. (You may have some left over.) Season the salad with salt and pepper. Spoon the avocado tomato mixture over the greens adding any juices collected in the bowl. Then sprinkle with queso fresco.

MARKET NOTE Queso fresco is a mild, moist, snow-white Mexican cheese that crumbles easily. It is sold in some grocery stores and Mexican markets. If unavailable, you can substitute feta.

CUMIN LIME DRESSING

2 TSP lime zest

1/4 CUP fresh lime juice

2 TSP minced garlic

1 TSP ground cumin

Kosher salt

Freshly ground black pepper

6 TBSP olive oil

SALAD

2 ripe avocados, peeled, pitted, and cut into 3/4-inch dice

1 CUP grape tomatoes, quartered lengthwise _or halved if small_

1/2 small red onion, thinly sliced

6 CUPS mixed torn Romaine

1/2 CUP crumbled queso fresco, plus more if needed _see Market Note_

SUMMER HEIRLOOM TOMATOES
IN CRUSHED FENNEL SEED DRESSING

PREP TIME	START-TO-FINISH	MAKE AHEAD
20 minutes	*50 minutes*	*Partially*

YOU CAN USE ANY VARIETY *of heirloom tomatoes in this salad. Reds like Cherokee Purple, yellows called Nebraska Wedding, orange varieties tagged Jaune Flame, and greens such as Green Zebras all work. And you can mix up the sizes, purchasing large orbs, slender oblong ones, and petite heirloom cherry tomatoes. The pairing of the tomatoes with a dressing scented with tarragon and crushed fennel seeds makes for an unexpected and delicious side for summer soups.*

FOR THE DRESSING, in a small nonreactive bowl, whisk together the vinegar, tarragon, mustard, fennel seeds, 1/4 teaspoon salt, and several grinds of pepper until well blended. Gradually whisk in the olive oil. (Dressing can be made 3 hours ahead. Cover and leave at room temperature. Whisk well before using.)

FOR THE SALAD, stem the larger tomatoes, and cut them lengthwise into 3/4-inch wedges. Halve or quarter any mini-heirlooms or cherry tomatoes. Place them in a shallow, nonreactive serving bowl and pour the dressing over them. Toss gently to coat. Let the tomatoes stand for 30 minutes or up to two hours, stirring occasionally.

TOSS the tomatoes well to distribute any liquid that has collected in the dish. Taste and season with more salt and pepper if needed. Sprinkle the remaining 2 teaspoons of tarragon over the tomatoes.

CRUSHED FENNEL SEED DRESSING

1 TBSP white wine vinegar

2 TSP chopped fresh tarragon

1/2 TSP Dijon mustard

1/2 TSP fennel seeds, crushed *see page 203*

Kosher salt

Freshly ground black pepper

3 TBSP olive oil

SALAD

2 LB heirloom tomatoes, including a variety of colors and size

2 TSP chopped fresh tarragon

MARKET SALAD
WITH FRESH PEAS, RADISHES & MELON

PREP TIME	START-TO-FINISH	MAKE AHEAD
25 minutes	*35 minutes*	*Partially*

ONE SUMMER IN FRANCE, *I tasted a version of this salad in a small restaurant on Cap Fréhel on Brittany's northern coast. What made it so memorable was the unusual mix of ingredients that included seasonal fruits paired with vegetables. At home, I prepared a close facsimile, using fresh peas, cubes of juicy cantaloupe, thinly sliced radishes, and local mixed greens from my farmers market. Tossed in a lemon vinaigrette and sprinkled with bits of goat cheese, this out-of-the-ordinary salad makes a perfect partner for warm or chilled soups in the spring or summer.*

FOR THE DRESSING, in a small nonreactive bowl whisk together lemon juice, vinegar, honey mustard, 1/2 teaspoon salt, several grinds of pepper, and sugar. Then whisk in the olive oil. (Dressing can be prepared one day ahead; cover and refrigerate. Bring to room temperature for 30 minutes and whisk well before using.)

FOR THE SALAD to a large bowl, add the endive, melon, radishes, and peas and toss gently with half of the dressing. Marinate 3 to 4 minutes. Add the lettuce greens and toss in just enough of the remaining dressing to coat lightly. (You may have some dressing left over.) Season the salad with salt and pepper generously.

GARNISH the salad with bits of chèvre.

MARKET NOTE When buying a cantaloupe, gently push in on the stem end; when ripe it should give to the touch. There should be a sweet smell as well.

LEMON SHALLOT DRESSING

2 TBSP fresh lemon juice

1/2 TSP red wine vinegar

1/2 TSP honey mustard

Kosher salt

Freshly ground black pepper

1/8 TSP sugar

1/4 CUP olive oil

SALAD

2 SMALL HEADS Belgian endive, halved lengthwise, and halves cut crosswise into 1/2-inch-thick slices

1 CUP diced (1/2-inch cubes) ripe cantaloupe *see Market Note*

3 radishes, trimmed and sliced very thinly

1/2 CUP (about 1/2 lb in pods) fresh shelled green peas

5 CUPS salad greens, such as baby romaine or mesclun

Kosher salt

Freshly ground black pepper

4 OZ firm chèvre, broken into small pieces

HARICOTS VERTS, CHERRY TOMATOES, AND CHORIZO SALAD
_IN_ SHERRY VINAIGRETTE

PREP TIME	START-TO-FINISH	MAKE AHEAD
15 minutes	_45 minutes_	_Partially_

WHAT MAKES THIS SALAD INTERESTING _is the topping of crispy bits of chorizo and chopped hard-boiled eggs that are sprinkled over a mélange of tender green beans, baby arugula, and cherry tomatoes. When I included this recipe at my annual salads class a few years ago, my students voted it their favorite, and it's one of mine, too. Satisfying and filling, it pairs well with light, chilled summer soups._

FOR THE DRESSING, in a large, nonreactive bowl whisk together the vinegar, mustard, 1/2 teaspoon salt, and several grinds of black pepper. Gradually whisk in the olive oil, then stir in the shallots. (Dressing can be prepared one day ahead; cover and refrigerate. Bring to room temperature for 30 minutes and whisk well before using.)

FOR THE SALAD, bring a large pot of water to a boil. Add the haricots verts and 2 teaspoons salt. Boil until tender, 5 to 6 minutes (or 2 minutes longer for tender young green beans). Drain beans in a colander and place under cold running water until cool. Pat dry. (Beans can be prepared 6 hours ahead. Cover and refrigerate. Bring to room temperature for 30 minutes before using.)

IN A MEDIUM, HEAVY SKILLET over medium heat, heat olive oil until hot. Add chorizo and cook, stirring, until lightly browned, about 3 minutes. Remove and drain on paper towels. (Chorizo can be prepared 2 hours ahead. Leave uncovered at room temperature.)

IN A LARGE BOWL, toss the beans and tomatoes with half of the dressing, and marinate 5 minutes. Add the arugula and toss again adding just enough dressing to coat lightly. Season with more salt and pepper if needed. (You may have some dressing left over.)

Arrange the salad on salad plates. Garnish each serving with a sprinkle of chorizo and chopped egg.

SHERRY VINAIGRETTE

2 TBSP sherry vinegar

1 1/4 TSP Dijon mustard

Kosher salt

Freshly ground black pepper

1/3 CUP olive oil

3 TBSP finely chopped shallots

SALAD

5 OZ haricots verts or tender green beans, ends trimmed

Kosher salt

1 TBSP olive oil

4 OZ Spanish-style chorizo, cut into 1/2-inch dice (_use Spanish-style chorizo in casing, not loose Mexican-style chorizo_)

10 cherry tomatoes, halved

4 CUPS (about 2 1/2-oz) arugula

Freshly ground black pepper

2 large eggs, hard-boiled and coarsely chopped

WINTER GREENS, ROASTED BEETS & WALNUTS
IN ORANGE DRESSING

PREP TIME	START-TO-FINISH	MAKE AHEAD
15 minutes	*1 hour, 45 minutes (including 1 hour 10 minutes for roasting the beets)*	*Partially*

THIS IS THE TYPE OF SALAD *that I see on bistro menus in Paris throughout the winter months. It's old fashioned, but always seems to be in style. This version calls for bright citrus accents of both orange juice and zest in the vinaigrette. Earthy roasted beet wedges, bits of creamy goat cheese, and toasted walnuts garnish the mixed greens of your choice.*

FOR THE DRESSING, in a small, nonreactive bowl, whisk together the orange zest and juice, vinegar, and a generous 1/4 teaspoon salt. Gradually whisk in the oil. (Dressing can be made one day ahead. Cover and refrigerate. Bring to room temperature for 30 minutes before using and whisk well.)

FOR THE SALAD, arrange a rack in the center position of the oven and preheat to 400°F. Pat beets dry, place in roasting pan, and toss with olive oil. Roast beets until tender when pierced with a sharp knife, about 1 hour, 10 minutes. Cool beets; then peel and cut off the roots. (Wear rubber gloves to prevent stains on your hands if you like.) Cut beets into 1/2-inch-thick wedges. (Beets can be prepared one day ahead. Cover and refrigerate. Bring to room temperature for 30 minutes before using.)

TO ASSEMBLE THE SALAD, set aside one tablespoon of dressing and set aside. In a large bowl, toss the mixed greens and walnuts with the remaining dressing. Taste the salad, and season with more salt if needed.

DIVIDE THE GREENS EVENLY among salad plates. Garnish each serving with beet slices then dot with goat cheese. Drizzle with a little of the reserved dressing and sprinkle with orange peel.

ORANGE VINAIGRETTE DRESSING

1 1/2 TSP grated orange zest

2 TBSP orange juice

2 TBSP white wine vinegar

Kosher salt

3 TBSP olive oil

SALAD

4 beets, 2- to 3-inches in diameter, unpeeled and scrubbed (all but 1-inch of tops removed but root ends left intact)

1 TBSP olive oil

6 CUPS (about 4 1/2-oz) mixed greens, cleaned and dried *red oak leaf, red and green leaf lettuce, and a small amount of frisée work well*

1/2 CUP walnut pieces, toasted *see page 203*

4 OZ chilled creamy goat cheese, broken into small pieces

Thin julienned orange peel *see page 203*

SHREDDED ROMAINE AND CUCUMBERS
WITH LIME DRESSING

PREP TIME	START-TO-FINISH	MAKE AHEAD
15 minutes	_35 minutes_	_Partially_

THIS SALAD, _assembled with a trio of greens that include romaine, basil, and mint, is tossed with a distinctive sweet and sour dressing. Fish sauce—a staple of Southeast Asian cooking—provides a salty taste, lime a sour or bitter note, sugar some sweetness, and red pepper flakes a bit of heat. The salad pairs especially well with Vietnamese- and Thai-style soups._

FOR THE DRESSING, in a medium nonreactive bowl whisk together the fish sauce, lime juice, sugar, garlic, ginger, red pepper flakes, lime zest, and water. (Dressing can be made one day ahead. Cover and refrigerate. Whisk well before using.)

FOR THE SALAD, peel the cucumber and halve lengthwise. Scoop out seeds with a spoon and discard. Thinly slice the cucumber and place in a salad bowl. Halve the avocado lengthwise, remove the pit and peel, then cut into 1/2-inch dice. Add to the bowl with the cucumber. Toss with 3 tablespoons of the dressing and marinate 5 minutes.

ADD THE ROMAINE STRIPS, basil, and mint to the salad bowl. Toss and add just enough of the remaining dressing to coat the greens. (You may have some dressing left over.) Sprinkle the salad with crushed peanuts.

LIME DRESSING

2 TBSP Thai fish sauce

2 TBSP fresh lime juice

2 TBSP sugar

1 medium garlic clove, peeled and grated

1 TSP grated fresh ginger

1/4 TSP red pepper flakes

1/4 TSP lime zest

5 TSP water

SALAD

1/2 medium cucumber

1 avocado

2 – 3 romaine hearts, cut crosswise into 1/2-inch strips _(to yield 6 cups)_

1/2 CUP loosely-packed, torn basil leaves

1/2 loosely-packed, torn mint leaves

1/3 CUP salted peanuts, crushed slightly

WATERCRESS SALAD
WITH ORANGE-GINGER DRESSING

PREP TIME	START-TO-FINISH	MAKE AHEAD
15 minutes	*20 minutes*	*Partially*

IN THE SPRING, *when my soups take on a lighter character and include such seasonal arrivals as asparagus, peas, and chives, this peppery watercress salad tossed in a bright orange-scented dressing is one I keep in mind. The dressing calls for less than a teaspoon of fragrant sesame oil, making it lighter than most, and gets a bit of subtle heat from freshly grated ginger.*

FOR THE DRESSING, in a medium nonreactive bowl, whisk together the vinegar, soy sauce, maple syrup, and sesame oil. Whisk in the orange zest and the ginger. (Dressing can be prepared one day ahead. Cover and refrigerate. Bring to room temperature for 30 minutes and whisk well before using.)

FOR THE SALAD, place the watercress and green onions in a medium bowl. Toss with just enough of the dressing to coat the leaves lightly. (You may have some dressing left over.)

MOUND the salad on salad plates and garnish each with some toasted sesame seeds.

ORANGE-GINGER DRESSING

2 TBSP rice wine vinegar

2 TBSP soy sauce

1 TBSP maple syrup

1/2 TSP toasted sesame oil

1 1/2 TSP grated orange zest

1/2 TSP grated fresh ginger

SALAD

1 LARGE (or 2 small) bunches watercress, cleaned and base stems trimmed *(to yield 6 cups of sprigs)*

4 green onions, including 2 inches of the green stems, sliced thinly on the diagonal

2 TSP sesame seeds, toasted *see page 203*

ARUGULA AND SHAVED FENNEL SALAD
IN LEMON DRESSING

PREP TIME	START-TO-FINISH	MAKE AHEAD
10 minutes	*45 minutes*	*Partially*

QUICK AND EASY, *this salad makes a great side to soups with strong, assertive flavors. The dressing is similar to one used for the Red Leaf and Belgian Endive Salad with Shaved Comté on page 114, but what a difference replacing balsamic vinegar with lemon juice makes. The citrus lightens the dressing, and turns it into a perfect foil for tangy arugula and anise-scented fennel.*

FOR THE DRESSING, in a medium nonreactive bowl, whisk together the lemon juice, mustard, scant 1/2 teaspoon salt, and several grinds of black pepper. Gradually whisk in the olive oil. Stir in the shallots. Taste and add more lemon juice if needed. (Dressing can be prepared one day ahead; cover and refrigerate. Bring to room temperature for 30 minutes and whisk well before using.)

FOR THE SALAD, with a sharp knife, halve the fennel bulb lengthwise, and remove and discard the tough inner cores from each piece. If you have a mandoline or a vegetable slicer, use it to shave the fennel into thin slices. If not, use a sharp knife to slice the bulb lengthwise into very thin julienne strips. Place the fennel in a salad bowl and toss with half of the dressing. Marinate 15 to 30 minutes.

ADD the arugula or lettuce greens to the bowl and toss, adding just enough of the remaining dressing to coat lightly. (You may have some dressing left over.) Season with salt and pepper if needed. If desired, sprinkle with walnuts.

LEMON VINAIGRETTE DRESSING

4 TSP fresh lemon juice, *plus* more if needed

1/2 TSP Dijon mustard

Kosher salt

Freshly ground black pepper

1/4 CUP olive oil

1/4 CUP finely chopped shallots

SALAD

1/2 MEDIUM fennel bulb

6 – 8 cups baby arugula, or a mix of arugula and tender baby greens

Kosher salt

Freshly ground black pepper

1/2 CUP walnuts, toasted and coarsely chopped *see page 203 optional*

GRILLED CHEESE TARTINES

GRILLED GOUDA AND KIELBASA
on rye

HAM AND CHEESE PANINI
with apple slaw

TUNA, HUMMUS, AND
KALAMATAS *on toasted multigrain*

GOAT CHEESE, RADISH, AND
ARUGULA PANINI

VEGETABLE PITAS *with whipped
feta and orange vinaigrette*

CHICKEN AND AVOCADO SALAD
CLUB SANDWICHES

TOASTED BAGUETTE, SMOKED
TURKEY, FONTINA, AND
GARLIC MAYO

SMASHED CHICKPEAS AND
ROASTED TOMATOES
on baguette slices

LOBSTER BLTS

CRAB SALAD SANDWICHES *on
toasted white*

CHICKEN SALAD WITH FENNEL
AND WALNUTS *on whole wheat*

7

SANDWICH SPECIALS

WHETHER TOASTED, grilled, served open-faced, or layered as a club, sandwiches help turn soups into meals. They provide the yin to the yang—something to crunch with something to sip. Although each can stand on its own, when sandwiches and soups join forces, they become more than the sum of their parts.

To this day I remember my first soup and sandwich pairing: cream of tomato soup (from a can) and grilled cheese (made with processed cheese). The grilled sandwiches in this chapter are far more interesting and wide-reaching, but no less satisfying than the combo I savored as a child. Deli-style Grilled Gouda and Kielbasa on Rye as well as Ham and Cheese Panini with Apple Slaw are two robust variations that make excellent partners to hearty vegetable or bean soups. And Grilled Cheese Tartines are a good choice to serve alongside light spring soups.

Vegetable lovers will appreciate the smashed chickpeas with roasted tomatoes served open faced on baguette slices, as well as the pita pockets filled with a crisp, chopped vegetable salad and whipped feta. Brightly colored and bursting with fresh tastes, they are ideal to serve alongside chilled soups in the heat of summer.

Many of these sandwich combinations feature pairings of unexpected ingredients. Tuna, Hummus, and Kalamatas on Toasted Multigrain elevates a classic tuna salad sandwich with unusual additions of hummus, cucumbers, mint, and olives. Goat Cheese, Radish, and Arugula Panini, a vegetarian option, is a light, refreshing rendition of the popular Italian sandwich.

Most sandwiches are best when made and served immediately. Keep this in mind, and time your soups to simmer or to be reheated as you prep, assemble, and in some cases grill the sandwiches in this chapter.

I've made suggestions for soup and sandwich pairings in the preceding chapters, but the real pleasure will come from composing your own duos. The sandwiches on the following pages are versatile enough to be mixed and matched effortlessly with the soups in this collection.

GRILLED CHEESE TARTINES

| **PREP TIME** | **START-TO-FINISH** | **MAKE AHEAD** |
| *15 minutes* | *30 minutes* | *Partially* |

MY FRIEND DEB SNOW, *the talented chef at Blue Heron Restaurant in Sunderland, Massachusetts, makes the best grilled cheese sandwiches I've ever tasted. Prepared with grated Gruyère and Grafton cheddar (a white cheddar from Vermont) that is mounded between slices of good white bread, these sandwiches are coated with melted butter, quickly pan-fried, then placed in the oven for several minutes. Deb cuts the sandwiches into squares or triangles and serves them with a simple balsamic sauce on the side. The sauce can be prepared a day ahead and warmed, and the sandwiches can be browned several hours in advance, then popped in the oven for a few minutes at serving time.*

FOR THE BALSAMIC SAUCE, in a small, heavy saucepan over medium heat, reduce the vinegar to 1/2 cup. (This should take 4 to 5 minutes, but can vary depending on your pan used so watch carefully.) Remove the pan from the heat, and whisk in the diced butter until mixture is smooth. Add extra butter to thicken the sauce if needed. (Sauce can be made 1 day ahead. Cool, cover, and refrigerate. Reheat just to warm over medium heat.)

ARRANGE A RACK at center position and preheat oven to 375°F.

PLACE 4 BREAD SLICES on a work surface. Toss the Gruyère and cheddar together, then divide the mixture evenly and spread on top of each slice. Top with remaining bread slices. With a pastry brush, use half of the melted butter to coat the top of each sandwich generously.

PLACE A LARGE SKILLET or griddle over medium-high heat. When hot, add enough sandwiches to fit comfortably in a single layer, buttered sides down. Brush the tops of the sandwiches generously with the remaining butter. Cook until the bottoms of the sandwiches are golden brown, 1 to 2 minutes, then turn and cook 1 to 2 minutes more. Transfer sandwiches to a baking sheet. Watch carefully so that the sandwiches don't get too brown. Repeat with remaining sandwiches. (Sandwiches can be prepared to this stage 3 hours ahead. Cool, cover loosely with plastic wrap, and refrigerate.)

PLACE the sandwiches in the oven to heat through and melt cheese completely, 6 to 8 minutes.

CUT EACH SANDWICH into 4 equal triangles or squares. Arrange tartines on a serving plate along with a small bowl of balsamic sauce for dipping.

MARKET NOTE Grafton cheddar, produced in Grafton, Vermont, is a superb aged white cheddar sold in many parts of the country. If it is not available, substitute another aged, sharp white cheddar.

BALSAMIC SAUCE

1 CUP balsamic vinegar, preferably one that is aged

2 TBSP unsalted butter, chilled and diced, *plus* **1 TBSP** *extra if needed*

SANDWICHES

8 SLICES best quality white bread, crusts removed

1/2 CUP (about 2-oz) Gruyère cheese, grated

1/2 CUP (about 2-oz) Grafton cheddar cheese, grated *see Market Note*

4 TBSP unsalted butter, melted

GRILLED GOUDA & KIELBASA ON RYE

PREP TIME	START-TO-FINISH	MAKE AHEAD
10 minutes	*30 minutes*	*No*

A VARIATION ON STANDARD *grilled cheese, these sandwiches are even heartier due to the addition of kielbasa and sauerkraut. For the best flavor, a good seeded rye is essential, as well as a quality Gouda or Jarlsberg. I like to serve these sandwiches with robust bean or winter vegetable soups.*

IN A LARGE, HEAVY SKILLET or grill pan over medium heat, melt 1 1/2 tablespoons each butter and canola oil until bubbling. Add four of the bread slices and toast on both sides until lightly browned, 1 1/2 to 2 minutes per side.

USE HALF OF THE CHEESE to top all the slices in the skillet. Then use half of the kielbasa and half of the sauerkraut to top two of the slices, adding the kielbasa first, then the sauerkraut. Top the sauerkraut with a generous smear of mustard and cover with the remaining bread slices in the pan, pressing down with a spatula. Grill, turning once or twice, until the cheese has melted and the sandwiches are warm. Remove sandwiches from the pan and cover loosely with foil. Repeat to make *2* more sandwiches. Halve sandwiches and serve.

MARKET NOTE Kielbasa is sold cooked, so the meat simply needs to be heated as the sandwiches are grilled. Turkey kielbasa works fine in this recipe.

3 TBSP unsalted butter

3 TBSP canola oil

8 SLICES seeded rye bread

8 OZ Gouda or Jarlsberg, or other good melting cheese such as a sharp white cheddar or Havarti, coarsely grated

6-OZ kielbasa, sliced about 1/4-inch thick *see Market Note*

2/3 CUP fresh sauerkraut, drained well

Coarse ground mustard

HAM & CHEESE PANINI
WITH APPLE SLAW

PREP TIME	START-TO-FINISH	MAKE AHEAD
15 minutes	*45 minutes*	*Partially*

THE ADDITION *of an easy and quick apple slaw makes traditional ham and cheese panini more interesting. The slaw, a combination of julienned Granny Smiths and shredded cabbage tossed in a cider vinegar dressing, provides tart and sweet notes and a bit of crunch. If you don't have a panini maker, a stove top grill pan can fill in. If you don't have either, a heavy skillet coated with a little oil will work.*

FOR THE SLAW, in a medium bowl, whisk together the vinegar, oil, sugar, mustard, and cayenne. Add the apple and toss well to coat. Marinate 10 minutes. Stir in the cabbage and basil. Season with salt to taste. (Slaw can be prepared 2 hours ahead. Cover and refrigerate.)

FOR PANINI top 4 of the bread slices with half of the sliced cheese, then with the sliced ham. Place several spoonfuls of the slaw on each sandwich and top with remaining sliced cheese, then cover with remaining bread slices. Brush the outside of each sandwich generously with oil.

IF YOU HAVE a panini maker, cook the sandwiches following the manufacturer's directions. Otherwise, brush a stovetop grill pan with oil (or coat a large, heavy skillet with a thin layer of olive oil) and place over medium-high heat until very hot. Place enough sandwiches to fit comfortably on the grill or in the pan, and weigh down with a heavy skillet or press with a metal spatula. Cook until the cheese has melted and the bread is golden brown, about 2 minutes per side.

REMOVE PANINI and cover loosely with foil. Continue in the same way, brushing grill or pan with more olive oil if needed, until all the sandwiches are cooked. Halve sandwiches and serve.

MARKET NOTE A good crusty loaf such as *pain de campagne* or *pain de levain* works well. If you use a round loaf and the slices are extra wide in the center, cut those slices in half and use the two halves for one sandwich.

APPLE SLAW

1 TBSP cider vinegar

2 TSP olive oil

1 1/2 tsp sugar

1 1/2 TSP Dijon mustard

SMALL PINCH of cayenne pepper

1/2 medium Granny Smith apple, unpeeled, cored, and cut into julienne strips about 1/8-inch wide and 2-inch long

1 CUP finely shredded green cabbage

3 TBSP chopped basil

Kosher salt

PANINI

8 BREAD SLICES, cut 1/4-inch thick from a country artisan loaf *see Market Note*

8 OZ thinly sliced Munster, white cheddar, Gruyère or other good melting cheese

8 OZ thinly sliced, best-quality ham

Olive oil for brushing on bread and for the pan

TUNA, HUMMUS & KALAMATAS
ON TOASTED MULTIGRAIN

PREP TIME	START-TO-FINISH	MAKE AHEAD
30 minutes	*40 minutes*	*No*

THERE ARE PROBABLY *as many versions of tuna salad sandwiches as there are cooks who make them. I particularly like this one, in which hummus stands in for much of the mayonnaise in the dressing, and Kalamata olives, cucumbers, and fresh mint bring Mediterranean flavor to the mix.*

IN A MEDIUM BOWL, stir together the hummus, mayonnaise, 1 tablespoon of the lemon juice, lemon zest, and cumin until blended. Stir in the olives, celery, and onion, then add in the tuna, tomatoes, cucumber, and mint, and mix well. Season the mixture with 3/4 teaspoon salt and several grinds of black pepper. Add up to 1/2 tablespoon additional lemon juice if needed.

DIVIDE THE TUNA SALAD and mound on 6 of the bread slices. Top with lettuce, then with the remaining bread slices. Halve sandwiches and serve.

1/2 CUP plain (not seasoned) hummus

3 TBSP good-quality (not reduced-fat) mayonnaise

1 TBSP lemon juice *plus more if needed*

3/4 TSP lemon zest

1 1/4 TSP ground cumin

GENEROUS 1/2 CUP pitted, chopped Kalamata olives

1/3 CUP diced celery

3 TBSP chopped onion

9 TO 10-OZ solid white albacore tuna, packed in oil or water, drained well

1/2 CUP unpeeled, seeded tomatoes, cut into 1/2-inch dice, drained well

1/3 CUP peeled, seeded cucumber, cut into 1/4-inch dice

1/3 CUP chopped mint

Kosher salt

Freshly ground black pepper

12 SLICES crusty, country-style multigrain bread, toasted

Crisp lettuce leaves, such as Romaine

GOAT CHEESE, RADISH & ARUGULA PANINI

PREP TIME
10 minutes

START-TO-FINISH
25 minutes

MAKE AHEAD
Partially

SEVERAL YEARS AGO *when our family rented a house in Provence for 10 days in July, we spent most of our time cooking and then eating outside on the small terrace that overlooked the countryside. For* déjeuner *one day, I prepared these Goat Cheese, Radish, and Arugala Panini. I spread slices of good peasant bread with creamy chèvre, added a layer of paper-thin radish slices, and then a mound of arugula. There was no panini maker in our kitchen, so I cooked the sandwiches in a heavy skillet coated with olive oil until the cheese melted and the bread was lightly browned and crisp. These sandwiches partner well with light spring soups or chilled summer ones.*

IN A MEDIUM BOWL, use a fork to mix the goat cheese and the lemon zest together until blended. (Goat cheese mixture can be prepared a day ahead. Cover and refrigerate. Bring to room temperature before using.)

SPREAD THE BREAD SLICES with the goat cheese mixture, and top 4 slices with a layer of radishes. If desired, sprinkle the radishes with fleur de sel, then add a mound of arugula. Cover with the remaining bread slices, cheese sides down. Press firmly so that the panini hold together. Brush the outsides of the sandwiches generously with oil.

IF YOU HAVE A PANINI MAKER, cook the sandwiches following the manufacturer's directions. Otherwise, brush a stovetop grill pan with oil (or coat a large, heavy skillet with thin layer of olive oil) and place over medium-high heat until very hot. Place enough sandwiches to fit comfortably on the grill pan or in the pan, and weigh down with a heavy skillet, or press with a metal spatula. Cook until the cheese has melted and bread is golden brown, about 2 minutes per side.

REMOVE PANINI, and cover loosely with foil. Continue in the same way, brushing grill or pan with more olive oil if needed, until all the sandwiches are cooked. Halve sandwiches and serve.

MARKET NOTE A good crusty loaf such as *pain de campagne* or *pain de levain* works well in this recipe. If you use a round loaf and the slices are very wide in the center, halve those slices and use the two halves for one sandwich.

5 OZ creamy goat cheese, at room temperature

1 TSP grated lemon zest

8 SLICES good quality peasant bread *see Market Note*

5 TO 6 MEDIUM radishes, thinly sliced

Fleur de sel *optional*

1 BUNCH arugula or watercress

Olive oil

VEGETABLE PITAS
WITH WHIPPED FETA & ORANGE VINAIGRETTE

PREP TIME
25 minutes

START-TO-FINISH
*50 minutes (including
15 minutes for the
vegetables to marinate)*

MAKE AHEAD
Partially

CHERRY TOMATOES, *bell peppers, and cucumbers
are among the vegetables that provide a burst of color
and plenty of crunch for the filling of these sandwiches.
Marinated in a fresh orange dressing, this chopped salad
is then spooned into pita halves that have been spread with
creamy, whipped feta. Be sure to use 6-inch pitas since they
hold the filling more compactly than larger ones.*

FOR VINAIGRETTE, in a medium nonreactive bowl,
whisk together the vinegar, orange juice and zest, and
1/2 teaspoon salt. Whisk in the olive oil. (Vinaigrette
can be prepared one day ahead. Cover and refrigerate.
Bring to room temperature for 30 minutes and whisk
well before using.)

FOR PITAS, in a large nonreactive bowl, toss tomatoes,
chickpeas, cucumber, pepper, onion, olives, oregano,
and greens. Set aside 2 tablespoons of the dressing,
then add the rest to the bowl of vegetables. Toss well
and marinate 15 minutes, stirring several times.

MEANWHILE, place the feta and cream cheese in
a food processor and pulse until combined. With
processor running, add the olive oil then the reserved
dressing. Process until the mixture is smooth,
30 seconds or more.

ON THE INSIDE of each pita half, spread one side
liberally with whipped feta. With a slotted spoon,
fill each pita with a generous 1/2 cup of the vegetable
mixture. Repeat with remaining pitas.

ORANGE VINAIGRETTE

2 TBSP
red wine vinegar

1 TBSP
fresh orange juice

2 TSP grated
orange zest

Kosher salt

6 TBSP olive oil

VEGETABLE PITAS

1 CUP red or yellow
(or mixed) cherry
tomatoes, halved,
or quartered if large

3/4 CUP chickpeas,
rinsed and drained

3/4 CUP diced, seedless,
unpeeled cucumber

1 SMALL red or yellow
bell pepper, stemmed,
seeded, and cut
into 1/2-inch pieces

1/2 CUP chopped
red onion

1/2 CUP pitted
Kalamata olives,
quartered lengthwise

1/2 TSP dried oregano

1 1/2 CUPS packed
mixed baby greens,
coarsely chopped

6 OZ crumbled feta,
preferably at
room temperature

2 OZ cream cheese,
preferably at room
temperature, broken
into small chunks

1/4 CUP olive oil

FOUR 6-INCH pitas,
whole wheat or white,
halved

SMASHED CHICKPEAS & ROASTED TOMATOES ON BAGUETTE SLICES

PREP TIME	START-TO-FINISH	MAKE AHEAD
10 minutes	*35 minutes*	*No*

SMASHED CHICKPEAS *scented with lemon along with roasted cherry tomatoes and onions pair beautifully as toppings for toasted baguette slices. Roasting the tomatoes and onions brings out the sweetness of both, while a sprinkling of rosemary and thyme adds a nice herbal accent. Light yet full of satisfying flavors, these open-faced sandwiches are good served with warm spring vegetable soups or with chilled summer ones.*

ARRANGE A RACK at center position and preheat the oven to 375°F. Oil a rimmed baking sheet.

PLACE TOMATOES, onions, and garlic on the baking sheet and sprinkle with thyme, rosemary, cayenne, 3/4 teaspoon salt, and several grinds of black pepper. Drizzle with 2 tablespoons of the olive oil and toss to combine.

ROAST UNTIL TOMATOES are softened and wrinkled, stirring several times, 15 minutes. (Watch carefully so that the onion and garlic do not burn.) Remove but retain oven temperature.

BRUSH BOTH SIDES of the baguette slices with olive oil and place them on another baking sheet. Bake 4 minutes. Turn and bake on the other side until bread is golden and slightly crisp, 3 to 4 minutes. Remove from oven, sprinkle lightly with salt, and cool slightly.

IN A MEDIUM BOWL, coarsely mash the chickpeas with a fork and stir in the 2 remaining tablespoons of olive oil, lemon zest, and lemon juice. Season with 1/2 teaspoon salt or more and several grinds of black pepper. Spread each toasted bread slice with some chickpea mixture, then top generously with some of the tomato and onion mixture, being sure to scrape up some of the herbs and seasonings with the vegetables.

4 TBSP olive oil, *plus* more for brushing

1 PT cherry tomatoes *a mix of red and yellow works well*

1/4 CUP chopped onion

1/2 TSP minced garlic

3/4 TSP dried thyme

3/4 TSP dried rosemary, crushed *see page 203*

GENEROUS PINCH cayenne pepper

Kosher salt

Freshly ground black pepper

8 baguette slices, cut 1/4-inch thick on a sharp diagonal so they are about 5-inches wide, or 8 slices crusty sourdough bread (halved if they are extra-wide)

1 3/4 CUPS chickpeas, rinsed and drained

1 TSP grated lemon zest

1 1/2 TBSP lemon juice

LOBSTER BLTS

PREP TIME	START-TO-FINISH	MAKE AHEAD
15 minutes	25 minutes	No

THE ADDITION OF LOBSTER *turns an everyday BLT into a show-stopping sandwich. For the base, I use a simple lobster salad inspired by my friend Brooke Dojny's fabulous filling for mini-lobster rolls. Only a small amount of bacon is called for so that it balances but does not overpower the lobster. This recipe can be doubled or tripled easily.*

IN A MEDIUM BOWL, whisk together the mayonnaise, lemon zest and juice, and tarragon. Use 3 to 4 teaspoons of this mixture to spread thinly on one side of each of the 4 toasted bread slices. Add the lobster and green onion to the remaining mayonnaise and mix well.

PLACE A LETTUCE LEAF on each of 2 bread slices. Mound half of the lobster salad atop each leaf, and sprinkle with the bacon. Top each sandwich with 2 to 3 tomato slices, and salt and pepper them well. Cover sandwiches with remaining bread slices, mayo sides down. Halve sandwiches and serve.

MARKET NOTE One pound of lobster will yield 3 to 4 ounces cooked meat. During the summer, some fish markets and grocery stores sell fresh cooked lobster meat, a great time saver. If you purchase cooked fresh lobster that has been frozen, defrost in the refrigerator overnight, and pat it dry with paper towels.

1/4 CUP good-quality (not reduced-fat) mayonnaise

1 TSP grated lemon zest

2 TSP lemon juice

1 TSP chopped fresh tarragon

4 slices good quality sourdough bread, lightly toasted

5 – 6 OZ lobster meat, cut into 1/2-inch pieces *see Market Note*

1 green onion, white and light green parts, chopped

2 leaves Boston or green leaf lettuce

2 bacon slices, fried until crisp, drained, and crumbled coarsely

1 TO 2 MEDIUM tomatoes, sliced

Kosher salt

Freshly ground black pepper

CRAB SALAD SANDWICHES
ON TOASTED WHITE

PREP TIME
10 minutes

START-TO-FINISH
15 minutes

MAKE AHEAD
Partially

THE CRAB SALAD *used as the filling for these sandwiches is the same one used as a garnish for the Red Pepper Velouté on page 36. I discovered by chance that it is just as appealing between slices of bread. The sweetness of the crab countered by a fresh citrus accent from the orange is the secret to its bright, refreshing taste. This sandwich is best when made with good-quality toasted white bread, so the taste of the shellfish remains the focus.*

IN A MEDIUM BOWL, whisk together the mayonnaise, sherry, and orange zest. Stir in the crab, green onions, and chives. (The crab salad can be prepared four hours ahead; keep covered and refrigerated.)

TO SERVE, generously top 4 of the toasted slices with crab salad, then with some mixed salad greens. Cover each with a remaining bread slice. Halve sandwiches and serve.

1/2 CUP good-quality (not reduced-fat) mayonnaise

1 1/4 TSP dry sherry

1 TSP grated orange zest

8 OZ fresh crab meat, picked over

3 green onions, including 2 inches of the green stems, chopped

2 1/2 TBSP chopped chives

8 SLICES good-quality white sandwich bread, toasted

1 CUP mixed salad greens

CHICKEN SALAD
WITH FENNEL & WALNUTS ON WHOLE WHEAT

PREP TIME
25 minutes

START-TO-FINISH
35 minutes

MAKE AHEAD
Partially

YOU CAN PUT *leftover roast chicken (including extras from a mildly seasoned rotisserie bird) to good use in this easy recipe. And for a delicious post-Thanksgiving sandwich, simply replace the chicken with turkey. Fennel (used instead of the typical celery) along with walnuts give the salad its crunch, while golden raisins offer a welcoming sweet note.*

IN A MEDIUM BOWL, whisk together the mayonnaise, mustard, lemon juice and zest, tarragon, 1/4 teaspoon salt and 3/8 tsp black pepper. Add the chicken, fennel, green onions, raisins, and walnuts. Mix well to combine. Taste and season the salad with more salt and pepper, and an extra squeeze or two of lemon juice if needed. (Chicken salad can be prepared 4 hours ahead. Cover and refrigerate.)

SPREAD THE CHICKEN SALAD evenly on 4 of the toasted bread slices. Top each with watercress sprigs or Bibb lettuce leaves, and cover with remaining toasted bread slices. Halve sandwiches and serve.

MARKET NOTE If using a rotisserie chicken, avoid those seasoned with strong flavors such as barbecued ones. Count on about 1 pound to yield 2 cups diced.

1/2 CUP good-quality (not reduced-fat) mayonnaise

1/2 TSP Dijon mustard

4 TSP lemon juice *plus* more if needed

1/2 TSP grated lemon zest

3 TBSP chopped fresh tarragon

Kosher salt

Freshly ground black pepper

2 CUPS diced cooked chicken *see Market Note*

1/2 CUP diced fennel

1/3 CUP chopped green onion, including 2 inches of the green stems

1/4 CUP golden raisins

1/4 CUP walnuts, toasted and coarsely chopped

8 whole-wheat bread slices, cut from a crusty artisan loaf, toasted

Watercress or Bibb lettuce

LIME AND GINGER CREAM
CHEESE BARS

THREE-LAYER CHOCOLATE
CARAMEL BARS

CHOCOLATE CASHEW BROWNIES
with chocolate crème fraîche glaze

CRISP OATMEAL THINS
SCENTED *with orange*

PUMPKIN BROWNIES
with maple cream cheese frosting

MOLASSES SPICE CAKE SQUARES

DARK CHOCOLATE PISTACHIO
BROWNIES *with chocolate glaze*

CHOCOLATE-AND-ALMOND-
STUDDED SHORTBREAD BARS

CHOCOLATE CUPCAKES
with almond crunch

"MELT IN YOUR MOUTH" LEMON
ROSEMARY COOKIES

ORANGE CUPCAKES
with white chocolate icing

BLUEBERRY PAN CAKE
with lemon crème fraîche

EXTRA EASY BROWN BUTTER
ALMOND CAKE

LEMON PUDDING "CAKES"

INDIVIDUAL SUMMER PEACH
CLAFOUTIS

CHERRIES POACHED
in red wine and spices

RUSTIC APRICOT TART

BUTTERMILK PANNA COTTAS
with blueberries

BUTTERSCOTCH POTS DE
CRÈME

CHOCOLATE AND CHESTNUT
POTS DE CRÈME

FLORENTINE SUNDAES

LEMON SORBET AND PROSECCO
PARFAITS

8

·············

DELICIOUS ENDINGS

NO SOUP SUPPER IS COMPLETE without something sweet at the end; but keeping it simple is my Golden Rule. All of the desserts in this chapter are homey and mouthwatering, and were chosen for their ease of preparation. Some can be made or baked while a pot of soup simmers atop the stove and will be ready to enjoy immediately. Others you will want to start earlier since they will need some time in the fridge. Ethereally light Crisp Oatmeal Thins Scented with Orange as well as "Melt in Your Mouth" Lemon Rosemary Cookies pair nicely with a bowl of fruit or fresh berries, but are equally tempting served alone to complete a soup supper. Lime and Ginger Cream Cheese Bars provide a cooling finish after spicy chili. For autumn vegetable soups, try Pumpkin Brownies with Maple Cream Cheese Frosting or Molasses Spice Cake Squares for a delectable, seasonally appropriate finale.

The cakes, tarts, and creamy baked puddings on the pages that follow belie the simplicity of their recipes, and will elevate any soup meal to the next level. Extra Easy Brown Butter Almond Cake, which takes only minutes to assemble and bakes in under a half hour, is so versatile you could serve it after any soup in this book. The colorful Rustic Apricot Tart, prepared with fresh apricots and almond paste, does not require a tart pan, making it as easy as it is delicious. French pots de crème in a duo of flavors—butterscotch and dark chocolate with chestnut—are quickly mixed and then need unattended time in the oven. Served in individual ramekins, these rich, silky smooth custards are crowd pleasers every time.

When you want to serve a really special dessert (even if you're short on time), try the Florentine Sundaes or the Lemon Sorbet and Prosecco Parfaits. Both require no cooking at all— just a quick assembly—and create a dramatic presentation for a few minutes of work.

While I've suggested pairings in the previous chapters, most of these desserts would work well with just about any soup you choose. So let the occasion and your taste buds be your guides. Deciding which dessert to serve might be the hard part!

LIME & GINGER CREAM CHEESE BARS

PREP TIME
20 minutes   **START-TO-FINISH**
1 hour, plus time for chilling   **MAKE AHEAD**
Yes

THESE SLIM BARS *are only about three-quarters of an inch high, but are packed with flavor. Simple, quick, and addictive, they are prepared with a crust of ground ginger snaps, sugar, and melted butter, all combined and packed onto the bottom of a baking pan. The creamy filling is made with a cheesecake-style batter enhanced with bits of crystallized ginger and a robust accent of lime.*

ARRANGE a rack at center position and preheat the oven to 350°F. Generously butter the bottom and sides of an 8-inch square baking pan.

FOR CRUST, in a food processor, combine the ground gingersnaps with the sugar and process until mixed well, about 30 seconds. Add the melted butter and pulse until just combined. Using your fingers, press this mixture firmly onto the bottom of the prepared pan. Bake 8 minutes, then remove the pan from oven and cool 15 minutes.

FOR FILLING, with an electric mixer on medium speed (and using the flat paddle attachment if you have one), beat the cream cheese until light and fluffy, about 3 minutes, stopping the machine and scraping down the sides of the bowl if necessary. Beat in 1/4 cup of sugar and the cornstarch until combined. Then beat in the egg and 2 tablespoons sour cream. Add the crystallized ginger, 1 1/2 teaspoons lime zest, and the lime juice, and beat until just combined. Pour mixture over the crust and smooth the top with a metal spatula or the back of a knife. The cream cheese layer will be only about 1/2-inch thick. Bake until a tester comes out nearly clean, about 25 minutes.

REMOVE THE PAN from the oven, but retain oven temperature. Whisk together the remaining 5 tablespoons sour cream, 2 teaspoons sugar, and 1/4 teaspoon lime zest in a small bowl. Then spread the mixture evenly over the top of the cream cheese layer. Return the pan to the oven and bake 5 minutes. Remove and cool in the pan; then cover and refrigerate for at least 2 hours or overnight.

WITH a sharp knife cut down all the way through the crust into 9 equal-sized bars. Use an offset metal spatula to remove the bars from the pan and arrange on a serving platter. If desired, garnish each bar with julienned lime peel.

CRUST

3 1/2 TBSP unsalted butter, melted, *plus* more butter for the baking pan

3/4 CUP packed gingersnap crumbs, made with 14 to 16 ginger-snap cookies ground finely in a food processor

2 TBSP sugar

LIME AND GINGER CREAM CHEESE FILLING

8 OZ cream cheese, at room temperature

1/4 CUP *plus* **2 TSP** sugar

3/4 TSP cornstarch

1 large egg

1/4 CUP *plus* **3 TBSP** sour cream

2 TBSP finely chopped crystallized ginger

1 3/4 TSP grated lime zest

2 TBSP fresh lime juice

Thinly julienned lime peel, for garnish *optional*

THREE-LAYER CHOCOLATE CARAMEL BARS

PREP TIME	START-TO-FINISH	MAKE AHEAD
10 minutes	*1 hour 15 minutes, plus time for chilling*	*Yes*

THESE SCRUMPTIOUS BARS *are composed of a tender, buttery crust, a caramel center, and a dark chocolate glaze. They can be prepared up to two days ahead, so they are a great choice for times when you don't want any additional last-minute work. You can cut them into 16 petite squares or into 9 larger ones. I love to sprinkle the bars with a little fleur de sel or sea salt right before serving since it brightens both the chocolate and caramel flavors.*

ARRANGE A RACK at center position and preheat oven to 350°F. Butter an 8-inch-square baking pan. Then, using a sheet of parchment cut 7 1/2-by-15 inches, line the pan so that it covers the bottom and extends over two opposite sides of the dish. (This will make it easier to lift the baked bars from the pan.) Butter the paper.

FOR THE CRUST, in a mixing bowl, cream the butter until smooth with an electric mixer on medium speed, then beat in the sugar and salt. Beat to blend well, 1 to 2 minutes, then reduce the speed to low and beat in the flour. Gather the dough into a ball and place it in mounds, about a teaspoon each, on the bottom of the pan. With your fingers, press to form a smooth, even layer, then smooth with a metal spatula or the back of a knife. Prick the dough with the tines of a fork. Bake until dough is just starting to color lightly, 18 to 20 minutes. Remove the pan from the oven, but retain the oven temperature.

FOR THE CARAMEL LAYER, place the butter and light brown sugar in a heavy, medium saucepan set over medium low heat. Stir constantly with a whisk until the sugar has dissolved and the butter has melted, about 1 minute. Add the condensed milk and salt. Whisking constantly, bring the mixture to a slight simmer. Cook, whisking constantly (never letting the mixture come to a boil) until it thickens and starts to pull away from the sides of the pan, about 10 minutes. It will remain a beige color and not darken, as most caramel sauces do. As the milk cooks, it will caramelize lightly on the bottom of the pan so you may see some flakes floating in the mixture. That's okay.

POUR THE CARAMEL over the pastry crust, smoothing it into an even layer with a metal spatula or the back of a knife. Return the pan to the oven and bake 10 minutes. Remove and cool to room temperature.

CRUST

6 TBSP unsalted butter, at room temperature, *plus* more for the baking pan

3 TBSP sugar

1/4 TSP salt

1 CUP sifted all-purpose flour

CHOCOLATE AND CARAMEL LAYERS

1 TBSP unsalted butter

1 TBSP light brown sugar

ONE 14-OZ CAN sweetened condensed milk

1/4 TSP salt

3 OZ bittersweet chocolate, coarsely chopped

1/3 CUP heavy or whipping cream

Fleur de sel or sea salt *optional*

CONTINUED ⇢

CRISP OATMEAL THINS SCENTED
WITH ORANGE

PREP TIME	START-TO-FINISH	MAKE AHEAD
15 minutes	*45 minutes*	*Yes*

THESE OATMEAL COOKIES *are thin and crisp, closely resembling those ethereally light French cookies known as* tuiles. *Sliced almonds and grated orange zest add extra layers of flavor to the oatmeal batter. A recipe yields about five dozen, but be forewarned—these cookies are addictive. I've seen a handful of guests polish off an entire batch at one sitting!*

ARRANGE A RACK at the center position and preheat oven to 325°F. Line two large baking sheets with parchment paper.

IN A MEDIUM BOWL, stir together the oats, almonds, sugar, flour, salt, and baking powder. In another bowl, whisk the egg, vanilla, and almond extract until blended. Add the egg mixture to the oatmeal mixture, and stir until mixed well. Add the butter and orange zest, stirring until combined.

USING A TEASPOON, drop the batter onto a baking sheet, spacing the cookies 2 1/2 inches apart. Have ready two cooling racks. Bake one sheet at a time, until the cookies have spread and are golden, 7 to 10 minutes. Watch carefully as they can burn quickly. (If you have two ovens, you can bake two sheets at a time.)

REMOVE THE BAKING SHEET from the oven, and slide the parchment with the cookies onto a kitchen counter. Let cool about 3 to 4 minutes until you can use a spatula to lift them (or peel them) from the parchment. Transfer the cookies to a rack to firm and cool completely, about 5 minutes.

CONTINUE IN THIS WAY with the rest of the batter, reusing the parchment paper. (The cookies can be made four days ahead; store them in an airtight container at room temperature.)

1 CUP old fashioned or quick-cooking rolled oats

1/4 CUP sliced almonds, toasted *see page 202*

1 CUP sugar

3 TBSP all-purpose flour

1/2 TSP salt

1/2 TSP baking powder

1 large egg

3/4 TSP vanilla extract

1/4 TSP almond extract

1/2 CUP unsalted butter, melted and cooled

2 TSP grated orange zest

MOLASSES SPICE CAKE SQUARES

PREP TIME
15 minutes

START-TO-FINISH
1 hour, 15 minutes

MAKE AHEAD
Yes

THE RECIPE FOR THESE DARK, MOIST SQUARES *studded with walnuts and raisins came to me from Kelle Quist, a talented personal chef in western Massachusetts, who told me that the original recipe was created by her grandmother many years ago. The combination of spices, paired with molasses and the surprise ingredient of brewed coffee, results in a beautiful blending of flavors. In fact, the only change I made to the original directions was to replace vegetable shortening with more flavorful sweet butter. The squares are good at room temperature, but even better when served warm. If you want to gild the lily, top them with scoops of good quality vanilla or ginger ice cream.*

ARRANGE A RACK at center position and preheat oven to 325°F. Butter and flour a 9-by-13 inch baking pan. Line the bottom of the pan with parchment paper, and butter and flour the parchment paper.

MIX TOGETHER 1 cup of the flour, baking soda, baking powder, salt, cinnamon, nutmeg, cloves, and ginger; set aside. In a mixer on medium speed, cream the butter for one minute. Gradually add the sugar, and cream until the sugar is well dissolved and mixture is light in color, about 3 to 4 minutes. (It will still be slightly lumpy; that's okay.) Stop the machine to scrape down sides of the bowl if necessary.

ADD THE EGGS one at a time, and beat well after each addition. Beat in the molasses until blended. Reduce the speed to low, and alternately add the flour/mixture in three additions and the coffee in two, beginning and ending with the flour mixture. Stop the machine to scrape down the sides of the bowl if necessary.

REMOVE THE BOWL from the mixer, and stir in the remaining 3/4 cup flour, the raisins, and the nuts until combined. Spread the batter in the prepared pan, smoothing the top with a spatula or the back of a knife.

BAKE UNTIL a tester comes out clean, 25 to 30 minutes. Remove and cool 15 to 20 minutes. Loosen the edges with a sharp knife and gently invert onto a work surface. Remove the parchment. Cut into 16 squares. Serve warm or at room temperature dusted with confectioner's sugar. (Squares can be made ahead; cool and store in an airtight container at room temperature for up to two days.)

MARKET NOTE Both sulfured and unsulfured molasses are available. For this recipe, the latter is best since it has a lighter and cleaner flavor.

6 TBSP unsalted butter, at room temperature, *plus* more for the baking pan

1 3/4 cups all-purpose flour, *plus* more for the baking pan

1 TSP baking soda

1/2 TSP baking powder

1/2 TSP salt

1 TSP cinnamon

1/2 TSP freshly ground nutmeg

1/2 TSP ground cloves

1/2 TSP ground ginger

1 CUP sugar

2 large eggs

3 TBSP unsulfured molasses *see Market Note*

1 CUP brewed coffee, at room temperature

1 CUP dark or golden raisins

1 CUP walnuts, toasted and chopped *see page 203*

Confectioners' sugar for dusting

DARK CHOCOLATE PISTACHIO BROWNIES
WITH CHOCOLATE GLAZE

PREP TIME	START-TO-FINISH	MAKE AHEAD
20 minutes	*1 hour, 20 minutes, plus time for chilling*	*Yes*

WHEN I SERVED THESE *special fudgy brownies at a fall dinner for my husband's freshman class at Amherst College, I watched them disappear in minutes. I made them with pistachios instead of the more usual walnuts, pecans, or almonds. And, I used orange zest in place of vanilla. You can make them up to three days ahead so there's no last-minute stress.*

ARRANGE A RACK at center position and preheat the oven to 350°F. Lightly butter and flour an 8-inch square baking pan. Then, using a sheet of parchment cut 7 1/2-by-15 inches, line the pan so that it covers the bottom and extends over two opposite sides of the dish. (This will make it easier to lift the cooked brownies from the pan.) Butter the bottom and sides of the paper and dust with flour, shaking out any excess.

PLACE THE BUTTER and the unsweetened chocolate in a heat-proof bowl set over, but not touching, a saucepan of simmering water. Stir until melted and the mixture is smooth and shiny. Remove from heat and cool 10 minutes.

WITH A WOODEN SPOON, stir in the sugar, orange zest, and salt. Add the eggs one at a time, stirring well after each addition until mixture is well blended. Add the flour and pistachios and stir well until no traces of flour remain.

SPREAD BATTER in prepared pan and smooth top with a metal spatula or the back of a knife. Bake until a tester inserted into center comes out with a moist crumb, 20 to 22 minutes. Do not overbake.

COOL BROWNIES in the pan. Run a sharp knife around inside edges of pan to loosen, then lift from the pan using the parchment paper as an aid. Cut into 16 small or 9 larger squares and place on a baking sheet.

FOR THE GLAZE, place the semisweet chocolate and cream in a heat-proof bowl set over but not touching a saucepan of simmering water. Stir constantly until the chocolate has melted and mixture is smooth and warm. If you have a squeeze bottle, transfer the warm chocolate to it, and drizzle in a zigzag pattern over the top of the brownies. Or, use a teaspoon to drizzle the warm chocolate over the brownies. Sprinkle the top of the brownies with pistachios.

REFRIGERATE THE BROWNIES until the glaze is set, 1 hour or longer. (Brownies can be prepared three days ahead; store in an airtight container in the refrigerator. Bring to room temperature before serving.)

DARK CHOCOLATE PISTACHIO BROWNIES

8 TBSP (1 stick) unsalted butter, diced, *plus* more for the baking pan

3 OZ unsweetened chocolate, chopped

1 CUP sugar

2 TSP grated orange zest

1/4 TSP sea salt, such as fleur de sel

2 large eggs, at room temperature

1/2 CUP all-purpose flour, *plus* more for the baking pan

1/2 CUP (2 oz) unsalted, shelled pistachios, toasted and chopped

GLAZE AND GARNISH

2-OZ semisweet chocolate, coarsely chopped

3 TBSP heavy or whipping cream

1 1/2 TBSP finely chopped pistachios

A squeeze bottle *optional*

CHOCOLATE-AND-ALMOND-STUDDED SHORTBREAD BARS

PREP TIME	**START-TO-FINISH**	**MAKE AHEAD**
15 minutes	*1 hour, 15 minutes*	*Yes*

FOR YEARS, *I bought decadent chocolate-and-almond-studded shortbread bars from one of the bakers at my local farmers' market. Although I used all sorts of ploys to get the recipe, the merchant shared only small tidbits. "Yes, they do have extra dark chunks of chocolate in them and, yes, there is a hint of sea salt," he confirmed, politely avoiding any other tips. After many attempts, I fashioned a close facsimile. The secret was to use 70% dark chocolate instead of the semisweet and bittersweet I first tried.*

ARRANGE A RACK at center position and preheat the oven to 350°F. Butter a 9-by-13 inch glass or ceramic baking pan. Dust with flour and shake out the excess.

PLACE THE FLOUR, both sugars, and sea salt in a food processor fitted with a metal blade. Pulse several times to blend. Then add the butter and process until mixture starts to come together and clump, about 1 minute. Transfer the mixture to a large bowl and stir in the chopped chocolate and almonds; mix well to combine.

PRESS THE DOUGH into an even layer in the prepared pan and bake until golden brown, 30 to 35 minutes. Cool in the pan for 15 minutes or longer, then cut the baked dough while it is still warm into 24 squares. (Halve the dough lengthwise and crosswise to yield 4 equal quarters and then cut each quarter into 6 equal pieces.)

LET THE BARS COOL in the pan, then, using a metal spatula, carefully remove to a serving plate. (The bars can be prepared two days ahead; store in an airtight container at room temperature.)

MARKET NOTE Lindt 70% dark chocolate, available in many supermarkets, works well in this recipe.

16 TBSP (2 sticks) unsalted butter, chilled and diced, *plus* more for the baking pan

2 CUPS all-purpose unbleached flour, *plus* more for the baking pan

1/2 CUP light brown sugar

1/2 CUP sugar

1 TSP sea salt, preferably fleur de sel

8 OZ 70% dark chocolate, coarsely chopped *see Market Note*

1 CUP whole almonds, toasted and chopped *see page 202*

CHOCOLATE CUPCAKES
WITH ALMOND CRUNCH

PREP TIME	START-TO-FINISH	MAKE AHEAD
10 minutes	*1 hour, 10 minutes*	*Yes*

Cupcakes are the last thing I expect to find at Parisian pâtisseries, but the French have fallen in love with this American bakery staple. Nowadays, many of the city's sweet shops display their own uniquely flavored versions, and I feel compelled to try them all! I discovered this dark chocolate, almondy gem during a long stay in the capital. The batter includes both cocoa powder and semisweet chocolate to produce a rich chocolate flavor, and in place of frosting, a creamy ganache is used as a glaze.

FOR ALMOND CRUNCH, line a baking sheet with foil. Stir sugar and 1 tablespoon water in a small, heavy saucepan over medium low heat until sugar dissolves. Increase heat to medium high and boil mixture without stirring until color is a rich amber brown, about 3 minutes. Remove pan from heat and add almonds, then pour the mixture onto foil and cool completely. Break into chunks, place in a plastic bag, and pound into a coarse powder using a rolling pin. (Almond crunch can be stored in an airtight container at room temperature for four days.)

ARRANGE A RACK at center position and preheat the oven to 350°F. Line a standard 12-mold muffin tin with cupcake liners.

FOR THE CUPCAKES, bring 1/2 cup water to a boil and remove from heat. Whisk in cocoa powder and chopped chocolate until smooth. In a medium bowl stir together flour, baking soda, and salt. With an electric mixer on medium speed, cream butter and sugar until light and smooth, stopping machine to scrape down sides of bowl as needed. Add eggs, one at a time, beating well after each addition. Reduce the speed to low and beat in 1/2 cup of the flour mixture. When incorporated, beat in 1/2 cup of the chocolate mixture. Continue, adding the flour and chocolate mixtures alternately, in half cupfuls. Stop the machine to scrape sides of bowl as needed. Stir in almond extract.

DIVIDE BATTER evenly among muffin cups and bake until a tester comes out clean, 18 to 20 minutes. Carefully remove cupcakes from tin to cool on a rack.

FOR GLAZE, in a small, heavy saucepan bring cream to a simmer. Remove from heat and whisk in chocolate until smooth. Cool 10 minutes and then transfer to a shallow bowl. Dip the tops of the cupcakes into the glaze swirling them to coat evenly and let the excess drip off. Sprinkle each glazed cupcake generously with some almond crunch. (You will likely have extra glaze or almond crunch left over; use it as a topping for vanilla ice cream.) Refrigerate until icing is set, then cover with plastic wrap. (Cupcakes can be prepared one day ahead. Store in the refrigerator and bring to room temperature 30 minutes before serving.)

ALMOND CRUNCH

1 /4 CUP sugar

1/2 CUP slivered almonds, toasted
see page 202

CUPCAKES

1/3 CUP Dutch process cocoa powder

3 OZ semisweet chocolate, coarsely chopped

1 CUP all-purpose flour

1/2 TSP baking soda

1/4 TSP salt

8 TBSP (1 stick) unsalted butter, softened

1/2 CUP sugar

2 large eggs

3/4 TSP almond extract

GLAZE

1/2 CUP whipping or heavy cream

4 OZ semisweet chocolate, coarsely chopped

"MELT IN YOUR MOUTH" LEMON ROSEMARY COOKIES

PREP TIME	START-TO-FINISH	MAKE AHEAD
10 minutes	1 hour, 30 minutes	Yes

Without fail, people love the assertive lemon flavor of these buttery cookies, which comes from the zest in the cookie dough and the lemon juice in the glaze. An herbal accent of fresh rosemary is more subtle, but is just as pleasing since it gently complements the citrus. These cookies are especially delicious when served with a bowl of fresh berries, peaches, or cherries.

ARRANGE RACKS in the center and upper thirds of the oven and preheat the oven to 350°F. Line two baking sheets with parchment paper.

IN THE BOWL of an electric mixer, cream the butter on medium speed until it is smooth, 1 to 2 minutes. Add sugar and vanilla and beat until completely incorporated, stopping the machine to scrape down the sides of the bowl as needed, about 2 minutes.

REDUCE THE SPEED to low and add the lemon zest, rosemary, salt, flour, and cornmeal. Beat until completely incorporated, stopping the machine to scrape down the sides as needed. The mixture should be smooth and resemble soft pie dough.

REFRIGERATE THE DOUGH in the bowl until it is chilled and firm, about 30 minutes. Then, scoop out scant 2-tablespoon-size portions and pat them into 1/4-inch thick disks. Place them 2 inches apart on the baking sheets.

BAKE UNTIL the cookies are beginning to brown around the edges, 12 to 14 minutes, switching the baking sheets from top to bottom after 6 minutes. Remove the cookies from the oven and carefully transfer to racks to cool. Set aside the baking sheets with parchment to use later.

FOR THE GLAZE, in a medium shallow bowl, whisk confectioners' sugar with the lemon juice until the mixture is smooth.

PLACE THE RACKS with the cooled cookies back on the parchment-lined baking sheets. Dip the top of each cookie into the glaze and swirl so that it covers the top, letting excess drip back into the bowl. Place the cookies, glazed side up, on the racks. Press a small rosemary sprig into the center of each cookie. Let stand until glaze is set. (Store the cookies in an airtight container at room temperature. Cookies can be prepared two days ahead.)

COOKIES

1 CUP (2 sticks) unsalted butter, softened

1/2 CUP confectioners' sugar

1/2 TSP vanilla

4 TSP lemon zest

4 TSP fresh rosemary, minced

1/4 TSP salt

2 CUPS sifted cake flour *see Cooking Tip*

1/4 CUP yellow cornmeal

GLAZE

3/4 CUP confectioners' sugar

2 TBSP lemon juice

Small rosemary sprigs for garnishing

COOKING TIP Be sure to use cake flour, which will give these cookies an extra tender bite, and measure the flour by sifting it into the measuring cup, then leveling with a table knife.

BLUEBERRY PAN CAKE
WITH LEMON CRÈME FRAÎCHE

PREP TIME	START-TO-FINISH	MAKE AHEAD
10 minutes	*1 hour, 15 minutes*	*Yes*

MARY WEBBER, *a friend and talented cook, shared the recipe for this simple blueberry pan cake with me, explaining that she had baked it for years, always to rave reviews. The cake is prepared with a classic batter of creamed sugar, butter, and eggs combined with flour and milk. Blueberries are coated in flour so that they bake suspended in the batter, rather than falling to the bottom. After the berries are folded in, the mixture is spread in a large baking pan rather than in a cake pan. I add a hint of lemon zest to the batter, and use buttermilk in place of regular milk for a tender crumb. The cake can be served warm or at room temperature, and serves 12 to 15 generously making it a perfect choice when you have a crowd.*

ARRANGE A RACK at center position, and preheat oven to 325°F. Butter and flour a 9-by-13 inch glass or ceramic baking pan.

FOR THE CAKE, sift together 2 2/3 cups flour, baking powder, and salt into a medium bowl and set aside. Rinse the blueberries in a large strainer and pat dry with paper towels. Dust the berries in the strainer with the remaining 1/3 cup flour, shaking off all excess flour.

WITH AN ELECTRIC MIXER on medium-high speed, cream the butter until it is smooth, 1 to 2 minutes. Add the sugar in a thin stream and beat until blended into the butter, 1 to 2 minutes. Add the eggs one at time, beating well after each addition. Reduce the speed to low, and add the flour mixture and the buttermilk alternately, beginning and ending with flour mixture. Beat in lemon zest and vanilla.

REMOVE FROM THE MIXER and fold in the blueberries. Spread the batter evenly in the baking pan. Bake until a tester comes out clean and the top of the cake is very lightly browned, 40 to 45 minutes. Remove and cool 10 minutes or longer. (The cake can be prepared 6 hours ahead; cool completely in the baking pan, then cover with plastic wrap and leave at cool room temperature.)

FOR LEMON CRÈME FRAÎCHE, in a serving bowl whisk all the ingredients except the mint together. (Lemon Crème Fraîche can be prepared one day ahead; cover and refrigerate.) Garnish the bowl with a mint sprig or two if you like.

SERVE THE CAKE warm or at room temperature, dust the cake with confectioners' sugar, and sprinkle with cinnamon. Cut into 12 to 15 portions, and serve each with a generous dollop of Lemon Crème Fraîche.

CAKE

11 TBSP (one stick *plus* 3 tbsp) unsalted butter, at room temperature, *plus* more for the baking pan

3 CUPS all-purpose flour, *plus* more for the baking pan

2 TSP baking powder

1/4 TSP salt

2 CUPS blueberries

1 1/3 CUPS sugar

2 large eggs

2/3 CUP buttermilk

2 TSP grated lemon zest

1 TSP vanilla

Confectioners' sugar, for dusting

Cinnamon, for sprinkling

LEMON CRÈME FRAÎCHE

1 1/2 CUPS crème fraîche *see page 201*

4 TSP grated lemon zest

4 TSP sugar

Mint sprigs for garnish *optional*

EXTRA EASY BROWN BUTTER ALMOND CAKE

PREP TIME
10 minutes

START-TO-FINISH
50 minutes

MAKE AHEAD
Yes

THE FRENCH *adore* financiers, *those mouthwatering little individual cakes made with brown butter, sugar, flour, and almonds. The confections are said to have originated in Paris's financial district, and take their name from the brokers (*financiers*) who bought them. My friend, Tina Isaac, who lives in Paris, introduced me to a simpler version of this classic treat. Her adaptation is to bake the batter in a single pan rather than in the traditional smaller molds. The batter can be assembled quickly and needs only about 20 minutes in the oven. Served warm with a dusting of powdered sugar, this golden cake is versatile. You can pair it with scoops of ice cream, a bowl of fresh berries, or drizzle it with your favorite chocolate ganache.*

ARRANGE A RACK at center position and preheat the oven to 450°F. Butter and flour an 8-inch cake pan, preferably one that is not dark (*see Cooking Tip*). Line the bottom with a piece of parchment cut to fit the pan. Butter and flour the paper.

PLACE THE BUTTER in a small, heavy saucepan set over medium heat. Whisk often until butter has melted and comes to a boil. Cook at a gentle boil until butter turns a rich nutty brown, 4 to 6 minutes. Watch carefully as the butter can go from brown to burning quickly. Remove from the heat and set aside to cool slightly.

PULSE THE ALMONDS in a food processor until they are finely ground. Transfer to a large mixing bowl and add the sugar, flour, and fleur de sel. Whisk to combine. Whisk in the egg whites and vanilla. Gradually whisk in the butter until well incorporated. Pour the batter into the prepared pan.

BAKE THE CAKE until golden and a tester comes out clean when inserted into the center, 17 to 20 minutes. Watch carefully so that it does not burn. (The cake will not be more than about an inch high.) Remove from the oven, cool 5 minutes, then unmold. Serve either warm or at room temperature. Dust lightly with confectioners' sugar.

COOKING TIP Because this cake cooks at an unusually high temperature, it is best to avoid dark metal cake pans. They tend to cook the sides of the cake too fast.

10 TBSP (1 stick *plus* 2 tbsp) unsalted butter at room temperature, *plus* more for the pan

1 CUP sliced or slivered almonds

1 CUP sugar

2/3 CUP all-purpose flour

1/4 TSP fleur de sel or sea salt

4 large egg whites at room temperature, lightly beaten

1 1/4 TSP vanilla

Confectioners' sugar

LEMON PUDDING "CAKES"

PREP TIME
10 minutes

START-TO-FINISH
50 minutes

MAKE AHEAD
Yes

This dessert is a cross between a pudding and an airy soufflé-like cake. The batter is prepared with creamed butter and sugar, plus egg yolks, lemon juice, milk, and a hint of flour, to which beaten egg whites are added. When baked, it divides into two distinct layers: a cake-like layer on top and a dense rich pudding on the bottom. I like these cakes best warm when their flavor seems more pronounced, but they are also tempting served at room temperature or chilled.

ARRANGE A RACK at center position and preheat oven to 350°F. Grease six 1/2-cup ramekins with butter. Set them in a large shallow baking pan.

ZEST AND JUICE the lemons to yield 1/3 cup lemon juice and 1 tablespoon packed zest.

WITH AN ELECTRIC MIXER on medium-high speed, beat together the butter and sugar until well blended, 3 to 4 minutes, stopping the machine to scrape down the sides of the bowl occasionally. Then beat in the zest. Reduce the speed to medium and beat in the yolks, one at a time. Gradually beat in the flour, again stopping to scrape down the sides of the bowl. Gradually add the lemon juice, then gradually add the milk. Mixture will be somewhat thin and may look curdled; that's okay.

WITH AN ELECTRIC MIXER on high speed and using clean bowl and beaters, beat the whites until soft peaks form. Mix 1/4 cup of the whites into the batter to lighten it. Then, in three equal additions, gently fold the remaining whites. Divide this mixture evenly among the buttered ramekins. Then fill the large pan with enough hot water to come halfway up the sides of the ramekins.

BAKE until a tester inserted into the centers of the puddings comes out clean, 18 to 20 minutes. The pudding cakes will puff up like little soufflés (but will not rise above the rims of the dishes) and will brown lightly on the tops. They will start to deflate after being removed from the oven.

REMOVE THE RAMEKINS from the pan. You can serve the pudding cakes warm, at room temperature, or chilled. (If serving chilled, cool, cover, and refrigerate them. They can be prepared one day ahead.) Garnish each serving with some fresh berries, a mint sprig, and a dusting of confectioners' sugar.

5 TBSP unsalted butter, softened, *plus* more for buttering the ramekins

2 TO 3 large lemons

3/4 CUP sugar

3 large eggs, separated, at room temperature

3 TBSP all-purpose flour

2/3 CUP whole milk

Strawberries, raspberries, or blueberries, for garnish

Confectioners' sugar, for garnish

Mint sprigs, for garnish

INDIVIDUAL SUMMER PEACH CLAFOUTIS

PREP TIME
15 minutes

START-TO-FINISH
50 minutes

MAKE AHEAD
No

Clafoutis, a specialty of the Limousin, an area in south central France, is one of the simplest yet most delicious French desserts a home cook can prepare. Traditionally made with cherries that are covered with a rich pancake-style batter then baked, this version calls for sliced peaches scented with hints of cardamom, ginger, and cinnamon. When baked, the batter rises slightly above the sides of the pan and then falls slightly like a soufflé as it rests.

ARRANGE A RACK at center position and preheat the oven to 350°F. Butter four 5 1/2-inch gratin or crème brûlée dishes and place them on a rimmed baking sheet.

DIVIDE THE SLICED peaches evenly among the dishes. Sprinkle the peaches in each dish with 1/2 teaspoon of the sugar.

PLACE EGGS in a mixing bowl and whisk well to blend. Whisk in the remaining 1/3 cup sugar, then the melted butter, then the milk. Sift the flour, cardamom, cinnamon, ginger, and salt over this batter and whisk until smooth. Stir in the vanilla.

POUR THE BATTER over the peaches in each dish and transfer them to the oven on the baking sheet. Bake until batter puffs up and rises slightly above the sides and has browned around the top edges, 25 to 30 minutes. Remove and cool 5 minutes; the clafoutis will deflate as they cool.

DUST THE CLAFOUTIS with confectioners' sugar, and serve warm.

2 TBSP *plus* **2 TSP** unsalted butter, melted, *plus* more for the baking dishes

4 (1 1/2 to 1 3/4 lb) large ripe peaches, peeled and cut into 3/4-inch wedges

2 TSP *plus* **1/3 CUP** sugar

2 large eggs

1/2 CUP whole milk

1/2 CUP *plus* **2 TBSP** all-purpose flour

1/8 TSP ground cardamom

1/8 TSP ground cinnamon

1/8 TSP ground ginger

Pinch salt

1/4 TSP vanilla

Confectioners' sugar for dusting

CHERRIES POACHED
IN RED WINE AND SPICES

PREP TIME
20 minutes

START-TO-FINISH
1 hour, 10 minutes

MAKE AHEAD
Yes

DURING THE SUMMER *when cherries are in season, I buy them often to eat by themselves. When I want to turn them into something special, though, I poach them in red wine, cardamom, and cinnamon. These two fragrant spices, plus a hint of orange, are all the seasonings needed. After the cherries are poached, I reduce the liquid to make a light syrup for the fruit. The glistening berries served over scoops of vanilla ice cream would make a fine finale for warm or chilled summer soups.*

PLACE RED WINE, sugar, cardamom, orange zest, orange juice, and cinnamon sticks in a 5-quart nonreactive, deep-sided pot over medium heat. Stir well to mix the sugar with the liquids, and bring the mixture to a simmer. Add the cherries and cook until they are tender when pierced with a knife, 10 minutes or more. Remove cherries with a slotted spoon to a shallow bowl or dish.

RETURN THE POT to medium-high heat and simmer until the poaching liquid has reduced, become somewhat syrupy, and coats the back of a spoon, about 30 minutes or more. Watch carefully so that the liquids do not become too thick. Cool the sauce 5 minutes, then return the cherries to the pot. (The cherries can be prepared two days ahead; cool completely, cover, and refrigerate. Reheat over medium heat, stirring gently, until cherries are heated through and sauce is warm, but not simmering.)

TO SERVE, ladle cherries and some sauce into six wide-mouthed wine or martini glasses. Garnish each serving with scoops of ice cream and, if desired, with a mint sprig.

COOKING TIP Cherry pitters, available in most cookware stores, are a good investment since they make pitting cherries a breeze.

---

4 CUPS dry red wine

1 1/2 CUPS sugar

3/4 TSP ground cardamom

1 1/4 TSP grated orange zest

1/3 CUP orange juice

TWO 3-INCH cinnamon sticks, broken in half

1 1/2 LB sweet cherries, stemmed and pitted *see Cooking Tip*

1 QT best-quality vanilla ice cream

6 mint sprigs, *optional*

RUSTIC APRICOT TART

PREP TIME	START-TO-FINISH	MAKE AHEAD
10 minutes	*2 hours, 45 minutes*	*Partially*

EMILY BELL, *my longtime assistant, created this freeform rustic tart. She rolls the dough into a circle, tops it with almond paste and then adds a luscious filling of fresh apricots tossed with lemon and sugar. The sides of the pastry are then lifted up to partially cover the fruit. When baked, the crust is golden brown and the apricots (which are dotted with butter) a glistening orange. The slightly tart fruit is balanced perfectly by the sweet almond paste. You can offer this dessert warm or at room temperature and, if you want some embellishment, top with scoops of vanilla ice cream or dollops of whipped cream. Don't expect any leftovers!*

FOR CRUST, combine flour, cornmeal, and salt in a food processor. Add butter and pulse, until mixture resembles coarse meal. With machine running, slowly add 3 tablespoons water. Stop machine to see if dough can be gathered easily into clumps. If dough is dry, add up to 1 tablespoon additional water and pulse a few seconds more. Remove dough, gather into a ball, and flatten into a disk. Wrap in plastic and chill 30 minutes (see Cooking Tip).

FOR FILLING, press almond paste into a disk, place between two sheets of waxed paper, and roll into a thin 8-inch round. Remove waxed paper, then place round on a plate and refrigerate uncovered to firm and chill, about 10 minutes.

HALVE THE APRICOTS lengthwise and pit. Cut halves into 3/4-inch wedges and place in a large bowl along with sugar, cornstarch, and lemon juice. Mix well.

PLACE CHILLED DOUGH between two sheets of waxed paper; roll into a 12-inch round. Sprinkle 1 tablespoon corn meal on a large unrimmed baking sheet. Remove one sheet of waxed paper and place dough (paper side up) on baking sheet. Remove other sheet of paper. Place almond paste on center of dough. Arrange apricots over almond paste and spoon any juices in bowl over them.

FOLD OUTER 2 INCHES of dough over filling to partially cover. Dot apricots in the center with butter. Chill 1 hour.

ARRANGE A RACK at center position and preheat oven to 400°F. Bake until crust is golden and apricots are bubbly, about 35 minutes. Remove and cool 10 minutes. If desired, sprinkle tart with sugar and serve with ice cream or whipped cream.

MARKET NOTE Almond paste is available in the baking section of most supermarkets. Odense, which comes in a 7-ounce tube, is one I use often.

COOKING TIP To make dough by hand, combine dry ingredients in a bowl. Blend in butter with a pastry cutter or two knives until mixture resembles oatmeal flakes. Gradually add water, mixing until dough just holds together. Gather into a ball. To ensure even blending of flour and fat, pull off about 1/4 of the dough and place on a floured work surface. Smear dough across the work surface and repeat with remaining dough. Gather pieces into a ball again and flatten into a disk.

CRUST

1 CUP flour

5 TBSP yellow cornmeal, *plus* extra for the baking sheet

1/2 TSP salt

1 STICK (4-oz) unsalted butter, chilled and diced into 1/2-inch pieces

3 – 4 TBSP ice water

FILLING

7 OZ almond paste *see Market Note*

1 1/2 LB fresh apricots, rinsed, and dried well

6 TBSP sugar

3 TBSP cornstarch

1 TSP fresh lemon juice

1 TBSP butter, diced

Confectioners' sugar for dusting *optional*

1 PINT vanilla ice cream or 1 cup heavy cream, whipped *optional*

BUTTERMILK PANNA COTTAS
WITH BLUEBERRIES

PREP TIME
5 minutes

START-TO-FINISH
30 minutes,
plus time for chilling

MAKE AHEAD
Yes

A CLASSIC ITALIAN DESSERT, *panna cotta (Italian for cooked cream) is a gloriously smooth custard made without eggs, bound with gelatin and served chilled. The recipe featured here is from Brian Alberg, chef at the Red Lion Inn in Stockbridge, Massachusetts. He cleverly uses buttermilk to add a bright tang to this confection, which keeps it from being cloying. Garnished with fresh blueberries and mint, this dessert is the answer when you want something that's quick, make-ahead, and delicious.*

SPRAY THE INSIDES of six 6-ounce (3/4 cup) ramekins or soufflé cups with non-stick cooking spray. Place gelatin in a small bowl and cover with 2 tablespoons water to soften, about 5 minutes.

IN A MEDIUM SAUCEPAN, whisk together the cream and sugar and place over medium-high heat. Stir until sugar dissolves and bring mixture to a simmer. Remove from heat and stir in the gelatin until it has completely dissolved, then stir in the buttermilk and vanilla. Transfer mixture to a large measuring cup with a spout and pour into the prepared ramekins.

PLACE RAMEKINS on a baking sheet or tray, cover with plastic wrap, and chill until completely set, 6 hours or overnight. (Panna cottas can be made two days ahead. Keep covered and refrigerated.)

WHEN READY TO SERVE, in a medium bowl toss blueberries, sugar, and lemon zest together. Have ready six dessert plates. Remove panna cottas from refrigerator and let stand at room temperature 10 minutes. To unmold, run a sharp knife around the inside edge of each ramekin. Fill a cake pan or pie plate with very hot water and dip the bottom of each ramekin in the water for about 10 seconds. Invert each ramekin onto the center of a dessert plate and gently lift off the dish. (If panna cotta doesn't release, dip again in hot water.) Garnish each serving with blueberries and a mint sprig.

PANNA COTTAS

2 TSP (1/4-oz envelope) powdered gelatin

3/4 CUP heavy cream

3/4 CUP sugar

2 CUPS buttermilk

1/4 TSP vanilla

GARNISH

1 1/2 CUPS blueberries

1 TBSP sugar

3/4 TSP grated lemon zest

6 mint sprigs

BUTTERSCOTCH POTS DE CRÈME

PREP TIME
10 minutes

START-TO-FINISH
*1 hour, 10 minutes,
plus time for chilling*

MAKE AHEAD
Yes

DURING A VISIT TO WASHINGTON, D.C. *at a restaurant called Ripple, I swooned over some butterscotch pots de crème that were served in ramekins topped with whipped cream and bits of toffee. What caught my attention was the silken texture and delicate balance of butter and brown sugar (the two ingredients which give butterscotch its flavor). After several tries, I had a version close to the original and just as indulgent.*

ARRANGE A RACK at center position and preheat oven to 325°F. Arrange six 1/2-cup ramekins in a large, shallow baking pan.

IN A MEDIUM SAUCEPAN (with a lid), heat cream until scalded and small bubbles form around the edge of pan (*see Cooking Tip*). Remove and cover.

IN A HEAVY 4-QUART SAUCEPAN over medium-low heat, melt butter and stir in the brown sugar. Stir constantly with a wooden spoon to prevent sugar from burning. Mixture will look lumpy at first and butter may separate, but continue to stir until it is smooth and glossy, 3 to 4 minutes.

TO THE SAME PAN gradually add the heated cream, 1 cup at a time. If sugar seizes into lumps, do not worry. Continue to stir, being certain to get into the corners of the pan, until sugar is dissolved and mixture is warm, 2 to 3 minutes. Remove and set aside.

WHISK EGG YOLKS in a large mixing bowl. Slowly whisk in 2 to 3 tablespoons of the warm cream mixture to temper the eggs. Whisk in remaining cream very gradually. Whisk in the bourbon, vanilla, and salt. Pour the mixture through a fine-meshed sieve into an 8-cup measuring cup or a large bowl, then pour or ladle into six ramekins.

POUR HOT WATER into baking pan to come halfway up the sides of ramekins. Tent the pan loosely with foil. Bake until custards are just set and centers are still a bit quivery, 30 to 40 minutes. (Check at 25 minutes that they are not done early.) Remove ramekins to a rack and cool to room temperature. Cover with plastic wrap and refrigerate until chilled, 2 to 3 hours. (The pots de crème can be prepared one day ahead.)

GARNISH each pot de crème with a dollop of whipped cream and toffee bits. Sprinkle lightly with cinnamon.

COOKING TIP Scalding the cream that is whisked into the melted butter and brown sugar mixture will help prevent it from seizing into lumps as it does when cream is cold.

POTS DE CRÈME

3 CUPS heavy or whipping cream

4 TBSP unsalted butter

3/4 CUP dark brown sugar, packed

6 large egg yolks

1 TBSP bourbon

1 TSP vanilla

1/4 TSP sea salt, such as fleur de sel

TOPPING

1/2 CUP heavy or whipping cream, whipped until soft peaks form

2 TBSP toffee bits

Powdered cinnamon

LEMON SORBET & PROSECCO PARFAITS

PREP TIME
5 minutes

START-TO-FINISH
15 minutes

MAKE AHEAD
Partially

SOMETIMES A DISH IS SO GOOD *that it remains in my memory long after I've tasted it. That was true of a dessert I tasted several years ago at Telepan on New York's Upper West Side. A delectable confection grabbed my taste buds and wouldn't let go. Scoops of lemon sorbet, softly whipped cream, and toasted almonds were alternately layered in glasses, and then topped with a generous pouring of Prosecco. At home I worked on my own version, adding some blueberries to the mix. Quick, easy, and delicious, this icy cold dessert will take only 15 to 20 minutes to prepare, but will be remembered much longer than that, thanks to the dramatic look of the Prosecco mixing with the layers of sorbet, fruit, and cream.*

WHIP THE CREAM to soft peaks and, if not using immediately, cover and refrigerate. (Cream can be whipped 2 hours ahead.)

WHEN READY TO ASSEMBLE THE PARFAITS, place a generous scoop of sorbet in a wide-mouthed glass. Spoon 2 to 3 heaping tablespoons of the cream over the sorbet. Sprinkle with blueberries and almonds. Make a second layering of sorbet, cream, berries, and almonds. Garnish the parfait with a mint sprig. Repeat to make 5 more servings.

OPEN THE BOTTLE OF PROSECCO and pour 3 to 4 tablespoons into each glass. The sparkling wine will bubble up and add a nice touch of foam to the parfaits. Serve immediately.

MARKET NOTE Be certain to use Prosecco, and not Champagne, because the latter is drier and doesn't provide enough of a sweet accent.

1 CUP heavy
or whipping cream

1 1/2 PINTS good-
quality lemon sorbet

1 CUP blueberries
*sliced strawberries will
work well, too*

1/2 CUP toasted almond
slivers *see page 202*

6 fresh mint sprigs,
for garnish

Chilled bottle of Prosecco
see Market Note

THE BASICS

STOCKS

Most soups rely on stocks to enhance their flavor. Whether it's chicken, beef, vegetable, or seafood depends on the recipe you are making. Using good stock ensures that a soup will taste its best, but that doesn't mean that every soup requires that you spend several hours making stock from scratch. I routinely use purchased chicken and beef stocks or broths, but am choosy about which ones I buy. (Swanson is my clear favorite, but yours might be another.) In my opinion, purchased vegetable and fish stocks are not as reliable and are better when enhanced.

Below you'll find my tried and true recipes for flavorful stocks. If you have plenty of time (and room in your freezer), you can prepare Homemade Chicken Stock, Beef Stock, or Vegetable Stock. If you are rushed but need an extra flavorful stock for a brodo (or for another soup where the quality of the stock is essential), try the Quick-and-Easy Chicken, Beef, or Vegetable Stock. These stocks are short-cut versions in which purchased stocks or broths are enhanced with vegetables and herbs. They take little more than half an hour to prep and simmer.

Fish stocks are in a category by themselves, as they are typically prepared with fish bones and shells (which are not always easy to come by), vegetables, wine, and water. For this collection, I have included a quick-and-easy one that calls for clam juice, white wine, and water simmered with vegetables and herbs. It works beautifully in soups like bouillabaisse.

For each of the soups in this book, I have suggested the type of stock or broth to use. Unless I recommend a homemade or a quick-and-easy stock (like the ones that follow), feel free to make them with stocks or broths from the market.

As I mentioned, stocks freeze well. Place them in a freezer container, label with the name and date, and store for up to three months. Having homemade or quick-and-easy stocks in your freezer is, in my view, as valuable as harboring a stash of solid gold.

HOMEMADE CHICKEN STOCK
(YIELDS 8 CUPS)

One 3-lb chicken, cut into pieces
2 medium onions, peeled and quartered
2 medium carrots, peeled and cut into 1-inch pieces
2 medium ribs celery, cut into 1-inch pieces
3 sprigs flat-leaf parsley
1 thyme sprig or 1/2 tsp dried thyme leaves
2 garlic cloves, crushed
1 1/2 tsp kosher salt

IN A LARGE, HEAVY POT, combine all ingredients and add 3 quarts of water. Bring the mixture to a simmer over medium-high heat. Lower the heat and simmer, uncovered, until the stock has developed a good flavor, 2 1/2 to 3 hours or longer. Spoon off and discard any foam that rises to the top while the stock is simmering. Add more water if the liquid cooks down below the level of the chicken and vegetables.

REMOVE THE POT from the heat and strain the stock through a large, fine-mesh sieve, pressing down on the solids to extract as much liquid as possible. Discard the vegetables, but save the chicken for another use if you like. Refrigerate the stock for 2 hours or until the grease has solidified on top. Then remove the fat with a spoon and discard.

TASTE THE STOCK and season with more salt if desired. (Stock can be prepared two days ahead; keep covered and refrigerated. It can also be frozen. Place in a freezer container, label with name and date, and store up to three months.)

QUICK-AND-EASY CHICKEN STOCK
(YIELDS 8 CUPS)

2 qt (8 cups) reduced-sodium chicken broth or stock, plus more if needed
2 ribs celery cut into 1-inch pieces
2 medium carrots, peeled and cut into 1-inch pieces
2 medium onions, peeled, halved, and cut into 1-inch slices
2 sprigs flat-leaf parsley
2 sprigs fresh thyme or 1/2 tsp dried thyme leaves

IN A LARGE, heavy saucepan or pot (with a lid) combine all ingredients and place over medium heat. Bring mixture to a simmer, lower heat, cover, and cook at a gentle simmer for 30 minutes.

STRAIN through a large sieve, pressing down on the vegetables and herbs to extract as much liquid as possible. Reserve the stock, discarding vegetables. You should have 8 cups. If not, add water to make 8 cups. (Stock can be prepared two days ahead. Cover and refrigerate. It can also be frozen. Place in a freezer container, label with name and date, and store up to three months.)

HOMEMADE BEEF STOCK
(YIELDS 8 CUPS)

2 pounds lean stew beef, such as chuck, cut into 1- to 2-inch cubes
2 pounds beef soup bones
2 carrots, peeled and cut into 1/2-inch pieces

2 large onions, peeled, halved, and cut into 1/2-inch slices
2 celery stalks, leaves included, cut into 1/2-inch pieces
1 cup dry white or red wine
2 tbsp tomato paste
3 sprigs fresh flat-leaf parsley
1 bay leaf, broken in half
1 clove garlic, crushed
1/2 tsp dried thyme
2 tsp kosher salt, plus more to taste

ARRANGE A RACK at center position of oven and preheat to 450°F.

IN A LARGE ROASTING PAN, place the beef cubes and bones, carrots, onions, and celery. Brown them in the oven for about 15 minutes, turning the vegetables once. Watch carefully, and if the vegetables start to burn, remove them.

TRANSFER THE BEEF and vegetables to a large 8-quart stockpot or deep-sided pot. Add the wine, tomato paste, parsley, bay leaf, garlic, thyme, and salt. Stir in 4 quarts water. Place the pot over medium heat and very slowly bring water to a boil. Then, reduce the heat and simmer, uncovered, for 3 1/2 to 4 hours, adding more water if the liquid cooks down below the level of the meat and vegetables. Spoon off and discard any foam that rises to the top while the stock is simmering.

REMOVE THE POT from the heat and strain the stock through a large sieve. Discard the meat, bones, and vegetables. Refrigerate for 2 hours until the grease has solidified on top. Then remove it with a spoon and discard.

TASTE THE STOCK and add more salt if desired. (Stock can be prepared two days ahead. Cover and refrigerate. It can also be frozen. Place in a freezer container, label with name and date, and store up to three months.)

QUICK-AND-EASY BEEF STOCK
(YIELDS 8 CUPS)

2 qt (8 cups) reduced-sodium beef broth or stock,
    plus more if needed
2 ribs celery, cut into 1-inch pieces
2 medium carrots, peeled and cut into 1-inch pieces
2 medium onions, peeled, halved, and cut into 1-inch slices
2 sprigs flat-leaf parsley
2 sprigs fresh thyme or 1/2 tsp dried thyme leaves

IN A LARGE, HEAVY SAUCEPAN or pot (with a lid) combine all ingredients and place over medium heat. Bring mixture to a simmer then lower heat, cover, and cook at a gentle simmer for 30 minutes.

STRAIN through a large sieve, pressing down on the vegetables and herbs to extract as much liquid as possible. Reserve the stock, discarding vegetables. You should have 8 cups. If not, add more water to make 8 cups. (Stock can be prepared two days ahead. Cover and refrigerate. It can also be frozen. Place in a freezer container, label with name and date, and store up to three months.)

HOMEMADE VEGETABLE STOCK
(YIELDS 6 CUPS)

2 medium onions, peeled, halved, and cut into 1-inch slices
2 medium carrots, peeled and cut into 1-inch pieces
2 medium leeks, white and light-green parts only, halved and
    cut into 1-inch pieces
2 ribs celery, cut into 1-inch pieces, leaves separated
    and reserved
4 plum tomatoes, quartered, membranes and seeds removed
4 oz mushrooms, halved (or quartered if very large)
6 garlic cloves, peeled and smashed
1/3 cup olive oil
2 tsp dried thyme
3 tsp kosher salt
5 sprigs fresh flat-leaf parsley
2 bay leaves broken in half

ARRANGE a rack at center position and preheat oven to 425°F.

SPREAD VEGETABLES on a large, rimmed baking sheet and drizzle with olive oil; sprinkle with thyme and 1 teaspoon salt. Roast for 30 minutes, stirring once or twice. (Some of the vegetables will be quite browned; that's fine.)

TRANSFER VEGETABLES and garlic to a large saucepan. Add 8 cups water, the celery leaves, parsley sprigs, bay leaves, and the remaining 2 teaspoons salt. Bring to a boil, then reduce heat, and cook, uncovered, at a gentle simmer for 45 minutes.

REMOVE POT from heat and strain stock through a large sieve, pressing down firmly on the vegetables to extract as much liquid as possible. You should have 6 cups. If not, add extra water to make 6 cups. Reserve the stock, discarding vegetables. (Stock can be prepared 2 days ahead; keep covered and refrigerated. To freeze, place in a freezer container, label with name and date, and store up to 3 months.)

QUICK-AND-EASY VEGETABLE STOCK
(YIELDS 6 CUPS)

2 qt (8 cups) vegetable stock or broth (preferably a light-colored one
   like Swanson)
2 ribs celery cut into 1-inch pieces
2 medium carrots, peeled and cut into 1-inch pieces
2 medium onions, peeled, halved, and cut into 1-inch slices
2 medium leeks (white and light green parts only) halved lengthwise and
   cut into 1-inch pieces
2 sprigs flat leaf parsley
2 sprigs fresh thyme or 1/2 tsp dried thyme leaves
2 bay leaves, broken in half

IN A LARGE, HEAVY SAUCEPAN or pot (with a lid) combine all ingredients and place over medium heat. Bring mixture to a simmer, lower heat, cover, and cook at a simmer 30 minutes.

STRAIN through a large sieve, pressing down on vegetables and herbs to extract as much liquid as possible. Reserve stock, discarding vegetables. You should have 6 cups. If not, add water to make 6 cups. (Stock can be prepared two days ahead; keep covered and refrigerated. It can also be frozen. Place in a freezer container, label with name and date, and store up to three months.)

QUICK-AND-EASY FISH STOCK
(YIELDS 6 TO 6 1/2 CUPS)

4 cups clam juice
3/4 cup dry white wine
1 medium carrot, peeled and cut into 1-inch pieces
1 celery stalk, cut into 1-inch pieces
2 bay leaves, broken in half
2 sprigs flat leaf parsley
2 thyme springs or 1/2 tsp dried thyme

IN A LARGE, HEAVY SAUCEPAN (WITH A LID) over medium heat, place all the ingredients and add 2 cups water. Bring to a simmer. Reduce heat, cover, and cook at a gentle simmer 25 minutes.

STRAIN through a large sieve, pressing down on the vegetables. You should have 6 to 6 1/2 cups. If not, add water to make 6 to 6 1/2 cups. (Stock can be prepared two days ahead; keep covered and refrigerated. It can also be frozen. Place in a freezer container, label with name and date, and store up to three months.)

COOKING TIPS, TECHNIQUES, AND HINTS

HOMEMADE CRÈME FRAÎCHE
(YIELDS ABOUT 1 1/3 CUPS)

Many supermarkets carry crème fraîche (a thick cream used in French cooking) in the dairy case or in the cheese aisle. If you can't find it, the following recipe works well.

1 cup heavy cream
1/3 cup sour cream

IN A MEDIUM NONREACTIVE BOWL whisk cream and sour cream together. Let stand at room temperature until thickened, 6 hours or longer. Cover and refrigerate. (Crème fraîche can be stored up to one week.)

TOASTED CROUTONS
(YIELDS ABOUT 2 CUPS)

2 cups bread cubes (3/4-inch dice), made from good-quality
   baguette or crusty country loaf
2 tbsp canola oil
1 tbsp unsalted butter

In a medium-sized heavy skillet over medium-high heat, heat the oil and butter until hot. Add the bread cubes; stir and cook until the bread is crisp and golden, 3 to 4 minutes. Remove and set aside. (Croutons can be prepared 4 hours ahead. Cover loosely with foil and leave at room temperature.)

TOASTED BREAD CRUMBS

(YIELDS ABOUT 1 CUP)

1/2 loaf peasant or country bread (sourdough works particularly well) with
   crusts removed
1 tbsp olive or canola oil

IN A FOOD PROCESSOR, pulse enough bread slices to make 1 cup coarse
crumbs.

HEAT THE OIL in a medium, heavy skillet over medium heat. When
hot, add the crumbs and cook, stirring constantly, until they are crisp and
golden brown, 3 to 4 minutes. (Bread crumbs can be stored in a plastic,
self-sealing bag and refrigerated for up to one week.)

TOASTING NUTS AND SEEDS

ALMONDS Spread nuts on a rimmed baking sheet and roast in a preheated
350°F oven until lightly browned, 6 to 8 minutes. Watch carefully so nuts
do not burn. Remove and cool.

CASHEWS Spread nuts on a rimmed baking sheet and roast in a preheated
350°F oven until lightly browned, about 6 minutes or longer. Watch
carefully so nuts do not burn. Remove and cool.

HAZELNUTS Spread nuts on a rimmed baking sheet and roast in a
preheated 350°F oven until lightly browned, about 8 minutes. Watch
carefully so nuts do not burn. Remove, cool, and place nuts in a kitchen
towel and rub off as much of the skins as possible.

PECANS Spread nuts on a rimmed baking sheet and roast in a preheated
350°F oven until lightly browned, 5 to 6 minutes. Watch carefully so nuts
do not burn. Remove and cool.

PEPITAS (PUMPKIN SEEDS) Place seeds in a skillet over medium heat.
Cook, stirring often until lightly browned, 4 to 5 minutes. (Seeds might
pop while they are cooking.) Watch carefully as they can burn quickly.
Remove and cool.

PINE NUTS Place nuts in a medium, heavy skillet over medium heat. Cook while stirring until nuts are lightly browned, 4 to 5 minutes or less. Watch carefully as they can burn quickly. Remove and cool.

SESAME SEEDS Place a small skillet over medium heat and when hot, add the seeds. Cook, stirring often, until the seeds are golden brown, 3 to 4 minutes or less. Watch carefully as they can burn quickly. Remove and cool.

WALNUTS Spread nuts on a rimmed baking sheet and place in a preheated 350°F oven until lightly browned, 6 to 8 minutes. Watch carefully so nuts do not burn. Remove and cool.

CRUSHING FENNEL OR CARAWAY SEEDS

Crush fennel or caraway seeds in a mortar with a pestle, or grind them in an electric spice grinder. Or, place them in a sealed plastic bag and pound them with a meat pounder or rolling pin. The seeds should be finely crushed unless the recipe calls for coarsely crushed ones.

JULIENNING ORANGE PEEL

Use a sharp knife or vegetable peeler to remove the orange's skin, without the bitter white flesh. Slice into very fine julienned strips.

SPECIAL INGREDIENTS

DRIED CRUSHED ROSEMARY—Save time by purchasing crushed dried rosemary, rather than whole rosemary leaves that you crush yourself. You can find them in the spice section of most supermarkets.

LEMONGRASS—These long slightly woody, grayish-green stalks about the size of green onions can be found in the produce section of many groceries and in Asian markets. Their slightly sour-lemon taste is an important ingredient in Thai and Vietnamese cooking. Store the stalks in a plastic bag for up to 2 weeks in the refrigerator. When using, remove and discard the tough outer layers, and then chop stalks finely.

SPANISH SMOKED PAPRIKA—Called pimenton, this paprika is available in gourmet food stores, in many groceries, and online. There is sweet (dulce), medium-hot (agridulce), and hot (picante). For the recipes in this collection, use the sweet variety.

INDEX

ACKNOWLEDGMENTS

It took more than a village to produce this book. My name might be on the cover, but it was the team effort of many talented people, near and far, that brought *Soup Nights* to life.

My agent, Lisa Ekus, and her staff, including Sally Ekus and Samantha Marsh, nurtured my idea for a soup book, and found a wonderful home for it at Rizzoli.

Emily Bell, my longtime assistant, was only a phone call away every time I confronted a new obstacle, and was the creative force behind many of the recipes.

Mary Francis, computer whiz par excellence, kept digital track of the recipes, charting them and sending them out to the testers, and then compiling all their comments.

Diana Tindall and Barbara Pitoniak tested recipes in my kitchen for a year, always offering candid wisdom. Longtime friends Sheri Lisak and June McCarthy fine-tuned recipes, suggesting improvements at every turn.

The recipe testers for this book cooked soups, salads, sandwiches, and desserts, week after week, and then took time to write detailed critiques. Special thanks to Marilyn Cozad, Wendy Ninke, Betty Orsega, and Ron Parent. I am also grateful to Marilyn Dougherty, Kent Faerber, Janet Hontanosas, Lorraine Hart, Julia Jackson, and Jackie Murrill.

Ellen Ellis and Carrie Harmon, both talented writers, made my words shine. Copy editor Amy Zavatto brought clarity and good judgment to the recipes and text.

Thanks to gifted photographer Harry Zernike, to creative food stylist Joy Howard, and to assistants Meaghan McGovern and Andiyah Patrick for the gorgeous photos. And my appreciation to Fred Leffel and Laurie Malkoff for opening their beautiful home for one of the photo shoots.

Peter Ahlberg designed a book that fulfilled all my wishes. Thank you for your attention to detail on every page and for the exquisite layout. And my appreciation to Kayleigh Jankowski for her patience and expertise with the final design editing.

There are not enough ways to say thank you to Caitlin Leffel, my editor, who oversaw, with an exceptional eye, every facet of this book's production. From organizing photo shoots to countless rounds of editing, she was focused, resourceful, and always encouraging.

Finally, to my husband, Ron, I say thank you once more (this is my 12th cookbook) for your support during this long project. "Merci" for sampling soups and sides nightly and for lending your professorial expertise to my words. You are the best.

FIRST PUBLISHED
IN
THE UNITED STATES OF AMERICA
IN 2016 BY:

RIZZOLI INTERNATIONAL PUBLICATIONS, INC.
300 Park Avenue South
New York, NY 10010
www.rizzoliusa.com

ISBN-13: 978-0-8478-4862-1
Library of Congress Control Number: 2016935019
Text © 2016 Betty Rosbottom
Photographs © Harry Zernike Photography

DESIGN BY:
AHL&CO
Peter Ahlberg, Kyle Chaille, Claudine Eriksson

Distributed to the U.S. trade by Random House, New York
2016 2017 2018 2019 2020 / 10 9 8 7 6 5 4 3 2 1

Printed in China